BOUTIQUE KNITS

BOUTIQUE KNITS

20+ MUST-HAVE ACCESSORIES

LAURA **IRWIN**

INTERWEAVE.
interweavebooks.com

Editor Anne Merrow
Technical Editor Karen Frisa

Photography Joe Hancock
Styling Carol Beaver
Hair and Makeup Kathy McKay
Technical Photography Ann Swanson

Interior Design Stacy Ebright
Cover Design Pamela Norman

Interweave Press LLC
201 East Fourth Street
Loveland, CO 80537-5655 USA
interweavebooks.com

Printed in China through Asia Pacific Offset.

Library of Congress Cataloging-in-Publication Data

Irwin, Laura, 1976-
Boutique knits : 20+ must-have accessories / Laura Irwin, author.
p. cm.
Includes bibliographical references and index.
ISBN 978-1-59668-073-9 (pbk.)
1. Knitting--Patterns. 2. Dress accessories. I. Title.
TT825.I79 2008
746.43'2041--dc22

2008010526

10 9 8 7 6 5 4 3 2 1

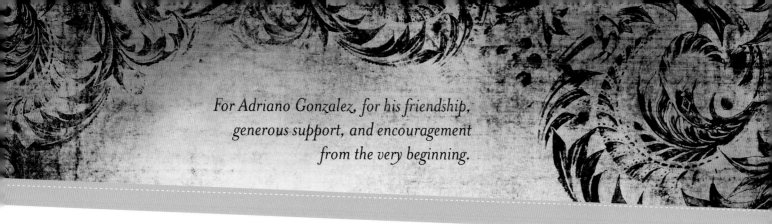

*For Adriano Gonzalez, for his friendship,
generous support, and encouragement
from the very beginning.*

ACKNOWLEDGMENTS

Thanks to the Interweave staff: Editorial Director Tricia Waddell, for taking a chance on me; Managing Editor Rebecca Campbell, for her sweet feedback that made me feel like I was getting it right; and Editor Anne Merrow, for her sense of humor and incredible knowledge.

Thanks to my knitters for their amazing attention to detail: Mary Bata, Anne Marie Gibson, and Jamie Sajovic.

Thanks to Church + State for allowing me to use pieces of their beautiful clothing for the photography of the book.

Thanks to the yarn companies who provided their lovely yarn for me to work with: Berroco, Blue Sky Alpacas, Brown Sheep, Classic Elite, Debbie Bliss, Elsebeth Lavold, Mission Falls, Muench, Plymouth, Reynolds, Rowan, SWTC, and Vermont Organic Fiber Company.

Extra special thanks to my mentors and teachers: Leigh Radford, for her friendship, generosity, knowledge, her tireless motivation, her enormous talent, the magical garden behind her house, and for showing me how it's all done! Dayna Pinkham, for her friendship, her open heart, her legendary talent, her modesty. Holly Stalder and Kathryn Towers, for their friendship, their genius, and for creating the boutique Seaplane, which first inspired me to knit and continues to push me to be a better designer. Suzanne Bartron, for being the original mentor and believing that I would eventually figure it out!

Super special thanks to friends Emily Bixler, Teak Wall, Brent Knoff, Tom Delaney, and Douglas Freeman, for listening to me talk about nothing but this book for a year solid and creatively knocking my socks off; to Erin Rackelman and Patricia No, for thinking my work was good enough to write about; to old-school Lint staff Melissa, Morgan, and Hillary, as well as all of the regular customers and students I've taught and who have taught me.

Love and thanks to all of my family, especially my parents, Sandy and Doug; my sisters, Ashlee and Michele; and my grandparents, Grammy and Grandma.

TABLE OF CONTENTS

INTRODUCTION
uncommon inspiration 8

PROJECTS

UNCOMMON INSPIRATION

Boutique Knits is meant to outfit women with an eye on fashion in a collection of stylish and curiously assembled accessories and layers. I picture the knitter who will be drawn to these projects: She insists on seeing her fashion sensibilities reflected in her handmade projects. She pays attention to the little details on all of her favorite pieces in her wardrobe. She is brilliant and quirky. She's got even better ideas than she knows. She is a designer or artist, although she may not know it yet.

The accessories of *Boutique Knits* introduce techniques, tools, and adornment rarely paired with knitting. These sweet patterns require a quick and clever mind, but not necessarily a lot of knitting expertise. When working on the patterns in this book, you will benefit most from a background in crafting, a healthy dose of improvisation, and impeccable attention to detail. These uncommon techniques and new materials will transform your knitting and give it a more complete and charming look.

What kind of uncommon techniques? Turning knitting on its side and working in a new direction. Using ribbing to turn a few unshaped geometric pieces into a curvy, clingy vest, and moving the bind-off to the front and center. Mixing felted and unfelted knits, not just for decoration but as structural elements. Knitting in pleats to create volume and dramatic decreases. Many of these projects use unique adornment like horse tackle, hardware, vintage lace, beads, ribbon, custom leather handles, grommets, and fabric-covered buttons.

I taught myself to knit, and I love to improvise. I really love being surprised at the end of knitting projects and enjoy teaching myself things. I hope these designs will surprise you and inspire you to improvise on your own!

PSEUDO SHIBORI SCARF

Shibori in knitting is often associated with felting, but you can manipulate knitted fabric without felting. Begin with a simple horizontal rib knitted on the bias, then use an improvised gathering and sewing technique for delicate but organic-looking results.

finished size
5½" (14 cm) wide and 66½" (169 cm) long before ruching; 5½" (14 cm) wide and 60" (152.5 cm) long after ruching.

yarn
Laceweight (Lace #0).
Shown here: Rowan Kidsilk Night (67% mohair, 18% silk, 10% polyester, 5% nylon; 227 yd [208 m]/25 g): #608 moonlight (gray), 2 balls.

needles
U.S. size 4 (3.5 mm). Adjust needle size if necessary to obtain the correct gauge.

notions
Tapestry needle.

gauge
22 sts and 36 rows = 4" (10 cm) in rib patt.

construction
The scarf is knitted diagonally in one piece. When main piece is completed, gathers are made with yarn and a tapestry needle. The scarf is completed by picking up stitches on the edges and working garter-stitch tabs.

stitch guide

rib pattern

Row 1: (RS) K1f&b, knit to last 3 sts, k2tog, k1.

Row 2: Purl.

Row 3: K1f&b, knit to last 3 sts, k2tog, k1.

Row 4: Knit.

Row 5: K1f&b, purl to last 3 sts, p2tog, p1.

Row 6: Knit.

Rep Rows 1–6 for patt.

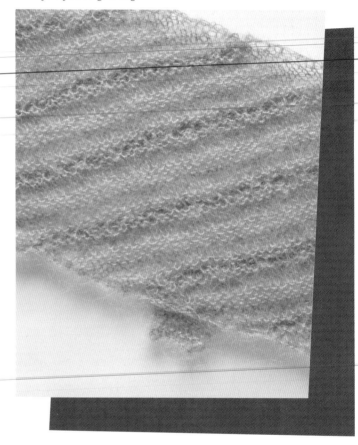

Back of scarf showing ruching

SCARF

CO 54 sts. Work in rib patt (see Stitch Guide) until piece measures 66½" (169 cm) from CO, ending with Row 2. BO all sts. Block lightly.

SHIBORI RUCHING

With yarn threaded on a tapestry needle and RS facing, beg at CO edge, locate the third rev St st (purl) ridge, pinch with fingers, and use running st (see Glossary, page 131) to sew St st (knit) troughs before and after it together, so that rev St st ridge bulges slightly. Repeat for every third rev St st ridge.

TABS

With RS facing and beg at CO edge, pick up and knit 8 sts on right selvedge between first 2 ruched rows. Work in garter st for 8 rows. BO all sts.

*Skip 5 spaces between ruched rows. In the sixth space, pick up and knit 8 sts on left selvedge and work tab as before. Skip 5 spaces between ruched rows. In the sixth space, pick up and knit 8 sts on right selvedge and work tab as before. Repeat from * once more—5 tabs total.

Weave in loose ends.

FAWN EARFLAP HAT

This hat was featured in my ready-to-wear line for Seaplane. Knitters are easy to spot in the shop—they pick up the knitwear and try to inspect it secretly—and I knew I had something special when two knitters came right out and asked to buy the pattern. It's so satisfying to finish a project in one day, and this one makes a darling impact.

finished size
18¾" (47.5 cm)
circumference.

yarn
Bulky weight (Super Bulky #6).
Shown here: Twinkle Soft Chunky (100% wool; 83 yd [76 m]/200 g): #26 lilac, 1 skein.

needles
U.S. size 15 (10 mm): 16" (40 cm) circular (cir) and set of 4 or 5 double-pointed (dpn). Adjust needle size if necessary to obtain the correct gauge.

notions
Stitch holder; size L/11 (8 mm) crochet hook; 2 yd (1.8 m) of 1½" (3.8 cm) wide satin ribbon, cut in half; two ⅜" (1 cm) pearl-like buttons; sewing needle and matching thread.

gauge
8½ sts and 13 rnds = 4" (10 cm) in St st.

construction
The earflaps are knitted separately, then joined and worked in seed stitch and stockinette stitch to shape the hat. Attach ribbons for ties.

HAT

first earflap

With cir needle, CO 3 sts.

Row 1: (RS) [K1f&b] 2 times, k1—5 sts.

Row 2: [K1, p1] 2 times, k1.

Row 3: Use the knitted method (see Glossary, page 127) to CO 1 st, purl st just cast on, [k1, p1] 2 times, k1—6 sts.

Row 4: Use the knitted method to CO 1 st, purl st just cast on, [k1, p1] 3 times—7 sts.

Row 5: [P1, k1] 3 times, p1.

Rep Row 5 for seed st until earflap measures 6" (15 cm), ending with a WS row. Place sts on a holder and cut yarn.

second earflap

Work as for first earflap but do not place sts on holder or cut yarn.

join pieces

Work 1 RS row across second earflap in seed st as established. Using the knitted method, CO 8 sts for back—15 sts.

With RS facing, work across first earflap in seed st as established.

Using the knitted method, CO 17 sts for front—39 sts.

With RS facing, place marker (pm) and join for working in the rnd, being careful not to twist sts. Work in seed st for 6 rnds.

Next rnd: K21, work in seed st to end of rnd.

Next rnd: K22, work in seed st to last st, k1.

Next rnd: K23, work in seed st to last 2 sts, k2.

Next rnd: K25, work in seed st to last 4 sts, k4.

Next rnd: K27, work in seed st to last 5 sts, k5.

Next rnd: K1f&b, knit to end—40 sts.

Work in St st for 8 rnds—piece measures about 5½" (14 cm) from joining rnd.

crown

Change to dpn when sts become too tight to work with cir needle.

Next rnd: *K6, k2tog; rep from * to end—35 sts rem.

Next rnd: Knit.

Next rnd: *K5, k2tog; rep from * to end—30 sts rem.

Next rnd: Knit.

Next rnd: *K4, k2tog; rep from * to end—25 sts rem.

Next rnd: *K3, k2tog; rep from * to end—20 sts rem.

Next rnd: *K2, k2tog; rep from * to end—15 sts rem.

Next rnd: *K1, k2tog; rep from * to end—10 sts rem.

Next rnd: [K2tog] 5 times—5 sts rem.

Pull tail through rem sts and fasten off inside.

FINISHING

With crochet hook and beg behind right earflap, sl st (see Glossary, page 128, for crochet instructions) around edge of brim and earflaps. Weave in loose ends.

Thread one ribbon halfway through the lower point of one earflap above the sl st edge. With needle and thread, sew button to ribbon, positioning button below wrong side of earflap, and sewing through both halves of the ribbon beneath the sl st edge. Rep for second earflap.

RS and WS of ribbons and buttons

BEST
FELTED COLLAR

Half felted and half unfelted, half angora and half wool, this scarf presents the best of both worlds. With the unfelted tie pattern in perfect garter stitch and the felted collar in an unfussy rib, this is an easy project for beginners to practice shaping. Wear it ascot-style or nestled against your throat.

finished size
collar: 12½" (31.5 cm) long and 5" (12.5 cm) wide before felting; 12½" (31.5 cm) long and 3¾" (9.5 cm) wide after felting; *garter ties:* 5¼" (13.5 cm) wide and 11½" (29 cm) long.

yarn
Worsted weight (Medium #4).
Shown here: Classic Elite Lush (50% angora, 50% wool; 123 yd [112 m]/50 g): #4478 auburn (reddish-brown), 2 skeins.

needles
U.S. size 8 (5 mm) and U.S. size 9 (5.5 mm). Adjust needle size if necessary to obtain the correct gauge.

notions
Two 1⅛" (2.9 cm) leather buttons; razor blade; tapestry needle; sewing needle and thread; pillowcase or lingerie bag with zipper.

gauge
17¾ sts and 35 rows = 4" (10 cm) in garter st on smaller needles. 22¾ sts and 22¾ rows = 4" (10 cm) in rib patt on larger needles before felting. 22¾ sts and 31 rows = 4" (10 cm) in rib patt on larger needles after felting.

construction
The collar is made in three pieces: two garter stitch ties and one felted collar. Cut the collar to attach the garter ties, then sew on the buttons for looks.

GARTER TIES (*make 2*)

With smaller needles, CO 31 sts.

Rows 1 and 2: Knit (1 garter ridge).

Rows 3–8: Using the knitted method (see Glossary, page 127), CO 2 sts, knit to end—43 sts after Row 8.

Rows 9–16: K1f&b, knit to end—51 sts after Row 16.

Work 14 rows in garter st (7 garter ridges).

Next row: (dec row) Ssk, knit to last 2 sts, k2tog—2 sts dec'd.

Next row: Knit.

Rep last 2 rows 3 more times—43 sts rem.

Next row: BO 2 sts at beg of row, knit to end.

Rep last row 5 more times—31 sts rem.

Work 2 rows in garter st (1 garter ridge). BO all sts.

COLLAR

With larger needles, CO 63 sts.

Row 1: (rib patt; RS) *K3, p1; rep from * to last 3 sts, k3.

Row 2: Work sts as they appear.

Rows 3 and 4: Using the knitted method, CO 4 sts, work CO sts in rib patt, cont in rib patt to end of row—71 sts after Row 4.

Work 22 rows in rib patt as established.

BO 4 sts at beg of next 2 rows, work in patt to end—63 sts rem.

Work 1 row even in patt.

With WS facing, BO all sts in patt.

FINISHING

felt

Place collar (not ties) in pillowcase or lingerie bag. With washing machine set to lowest water level, shortest cycle, and hottest temperature, wash the collar. (See Felt & Form, right, for information on felting.) Check piece for degree of felting every 5 minutes; if necessary, reset the washing machine to begin again, but do not allow the piece to go through a rinse or spin cycle. When it is sufficiently felted, remove the piece from the washer and shape to measurements. Allow to dry completely.

attach ties

Locate center of end of collar. Insert razor blade tip about ¾" (2 cm) from end and create ½" (1.3 cm) slit. Pull 1½" (3.8 cm) of one end of one garter tie through slit from RS to WS of collar. With yarn threaded on a tapestry needle, whipstitch (see Glossary, page 131) end of garter tie to itself on WS of tie. Sew button to felted collar next to (not on top of) slit. Create slit and attach second tie to other end of collar in same manner.

Front and back of collar with ties attached

FELT & FORM

Transforming your knitted piece of fabric into dense and durable felt requires only time in your washing machine and a few basic techniques. Look at the difference in density, texture, and stitch definition between the center and ties of the Best Felted Collar—they hardly seem to be made of the same raw material.

To keep the pieces from tangling up or stretching out, place them in a zippered pillowcase or lingerie bag. Put the bag or pillowcase in a washing machine set to the lowest water level, shortest cycle, and hottest temperature, and add a little laundry soap. It also helps to put an old pair of jeans or a tennis shoe in with the knitted pieces for extra agitation.

Wash the pieces, stopping the machine and pulling out the knits every 5 minutes to see whether the stitches have begun to disappear and the piece has shrunk to the desired size. If necessary, reset the washing machine to begin again, but do not allow the piece to go through a rinse or spin cycle, which can distort knitted fabric. (If the piece is really soapy, rinse it gently in warm water.)

When the pieces have shrunk to the desired size and you are satisfied with the feel of the fabric, pull them out of the washer. They will be sopping wet, so have towels at the ready. Roll the pieces in the towels and gently squeeze out the water.

The secret of beautiful felted knits is that in order to get the shape you want, you have to create it after you've finished knitting and felting. Sometimes you need a little extra help, like props to keep the desired shape and look. (I've used plastic bags, towels, and cardboard cutouts placed inside of plastic bags to keep the shape.) Lay the pieces out to dry on a clean towel, stretching them if necessary to the desired measurements. When the felt is dry, it will stay the shape and size it was when wet, so spend time molding and stretching the knitted felted piece for maximum beauty. Allow to dry completely; this may take several days.

SOFTLY PLEATED SLEEVES

Here is a pair of super-lush sleeves to rest your head upon while daydreaming in the colder months. The Victorian-style lace trim is appliquéd after the sleeves are completed. Who knew bamboo and alpaca could make such a desirable pairing?

finished size
10" (25.5 cm) long and 7" (18 cm) hand circumference. To fit woman's size small to medium.

yarn
DK weight (Light #3). *Shown here:* Blue Sky Alpacas Brushed Suri (67% baby suri alpaca, 22% merino wool, 11% bamboo; 142 yd [130 m]/50 g): #905 Earl Grey, 1 skein.

needles
U.S. size 6 (4 mm) and U.S. size 7 (4.5 mm): set of 5 double-pointed (dpn). Adjust needle size if necessary to obtain the correct gauge.

notions
Marker (m); ½ yd (.5 m) beaded trim (see Sources, page 134); sewing needle and thread to match trim; tapestry needle.

gauge
20½ sts and 31 rnds = 4" (10 cm) in St st on smaller needles.

construction
Each sleeve is worked in one piece, beginning flat with the hand-opening pleat and then worked in the round to the cuff. Purchased trim is sewn on after each sleeve is completed.

Trim folded in half to be sewn at center

SLEEVE

CO 20 sts on 1 smaller needle. Do not join.

Row 1: K1, ssk, knit to last 3 sts, k2tog, k1—18 sts rem.

Row 2: Purl.

Row 3: Rep Row 1—16 sts rem.

Row 4: With WS facing and using the knitted method (see Glossary, page 127), CO 18 sts onto an empty needle, place marker (pm), CO 18 sts onto another empty needle—52 sts total.

Turn work so RS is facing and join for working in the rnd, being careful not to twist sts. Knit to marker (beg of rnd).

Work 8 more rnds in St st.

make pleat

Next row: K10, hold rem 8 sts on needle in front of first 8 sts on next needle; with an empty needle, [knit first st on front needle tog with first st on back needle] 8 times, hold rem 8 sts on needle in back of first 8 sts on next needle, [knit first st on front needle tog with first st on back needle] 8 times, knit to end of rnd—36 sts rem.

arm

Work even in St st until piece measures 8" (20.5 cm) from pleat. Change to larger needles. Work in St st for 3 rnds. Loosely BO all sts.

FINISHING

Cut trim into 2 even lengths. Fold each piece in half as indicated and use sewing needle and thread to whipstitch (see Glossary, page 131) trim together at center. Beg at fold, pin trim to sleeve ¾" (1.3 cm) from CO of pleat. With sewing needle and thread, backstitch (see Glossary, page 130) top, bottom, and sides of trim in place. Weave in loose ends.

SILKY WOOL VEST

Purposely designed to look shapely without any knitted shaping, this vest is a perfect starter sweater project. By sewing on bridal button loops (found at fabric stores) at finishing, you can use just the right number of buttons without planning ahead for buttonholes.

finished size
28¾ (34, 39¼)" (73 [86.5, 99.5] cm) bust circumference. Vest shown measures 28¾" (73 cm). *Note:* Ribbed fabric will stretch considerably.

yarn
DK weight (Light #3).
Shown here: Elsebeth Lavold Silky Wool (65% wool, 35% silk; 192 yd [176 m]/50 g): #20 teal, 3 (4, 5) skeins.

needles
U.S. sizes 5 (3.75 mm) and 6 (4 mm): 24" (60 cm) circular (cir). Adjust needle size if necessary to obtain the correct gauge.

notions
Stitch holder; markers (m); twenty-eight (thirty-two, thirty-eight) $^7/_{16}$" (1.1 cm) buttons; 28 (32, 38) loops (about 15 [18, 20]" [38 (45.5, 51) cm]) white button-loop tape, cut in half; sewing needle and matching thread; sewing pins; tapestry needle.

gauge
28 sts and 33 rows = 4" (10 cm) in k2, p2 rib on larger needle.

construction
The vest is worked from the bottom up in one piece. The front is bound off and the back is worked to the back neck, then divided into two straps. The straps are worked long enough to wrap over the shoulders and attach to the front with buttons and loop tape.

stitch guide

Make bobble (MB): (Knit, purl, knit, purl) into the same st (4 new sts on right needle), pass first 3 sts over last st on right needle—1 st rem.

BODY

With smaller needle, CO 192 (224, 256) sts. Place marker (pm) and join for working in the rnd, being careful not to twist sts.

Set-up rnd: K1, p2, [k2, p2] 23 (27, 31) times, k1, pm, k1, p2, [k2, p2] 23 (27, 31) times, k1.

Work even in patt, working sts as they appear and slipping markers, until piece measures 1½" (3.8 cm). Change to larger needle.

Rnds 1–4: *K1, p2, [k2, p2] 9 (10, 11) times, k18 (26, 34), [p2, k2] 9 (10, 11) times, p2, k1, sl m; rep from * once more.

Rnd 5: (bobble rnd) K1, p2, [k2, p2] 9 (10, 11) times, k2, MB, k12 (20, 28), MB, k2, [p2, k2] 9 (10, 11) times, p2, k1, sl m, k1, p2, [k2, p2] 9 (10, 11) times, k18 (26, 34), [p2, k2] 9 (10, 11) times, p2, k1.

Rep Rnds 1–5 four (four, five) more times, then rep Rnds 1–4 once more—piece measures about 5 (5, 5½)" (12.5 [12.5, 14] cm) from CO.

Next rnd: BO 96 (112, 128) sts in patt for front, work to end of rnd in patt—96 (112, 128) sts rem for back.

back

Working back and forth in rows, work even in patt as established until piece measures 11 (12, 12½)" (28 [30.5, 31.5] cm) from CO, ending with a WS row.

right shoulder

Next row: (RS) K1, [p2, k2] 11 (13, 15) times, p2, k1, place next 48 (56, 64) sts on a holder for left shoulder—48 (56, 64) sts rem for right shoulder.

Work in patt as established until piece measures 16 (17, 18)" (40.5 [43, 45.5] cm) from neck division, ending with a WS row. BO all sts in patt.

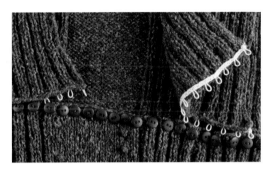

Sew button trim and buttons to vest bind-off edges.

left shoulder

Replace 48 (56, 64) held left shoulder sts onto larger needle. Rejoin yarn.

Next row: (RS) K1, p2, [k2, p2] 11 (13, 15) times, k1.

Work in patt as established until piece measures 16 (17, 18)" (40.5 [43, 45.5] cm) from neck division, ending with a WS row. BO all sts in patt.

FINISHING

Pin one piece of button-loop tape in place at end of WS of each shoulder piece. With sewing needle and thread, use running st (see Glossary, page 131) to sew tape in place. Sew 28 (32, 38) buttons to RS of front BO edge to correspond with loops. Weave in loose ends.

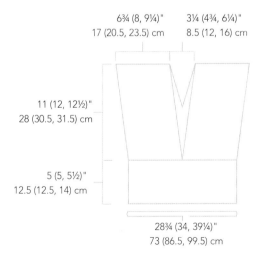

6¾ (8, 9¼)"
17 (20.5, 23.5) cm

3¼ (4¾, 6¼)"
8.5 (12, 16) cm

11 (12, 12½)"
28 (30.5, 31.5) cm

5 (5, 5½)"
12.5 (12.5, 14) cm

28¾ (34, 39¼)"
73 (86.5, 99.5) cm

SUNSHINE INTARSIA BAG

Beginning with a deep orange shade at the base, the color of this bag changes gradually with intarsia for a subtle transition to gold. After the pieces are sewn together and felted, a large D-ring (ordinarily used for horse tackle or leather work) is attached for a handle, secured in place with Chicago screws.

finished size

Before felting and seaming: Bag, 5½" (14 cm) wide at top, 13½" (34.5 cm) wide at widest point, 15½" (39.5 cm) tall; gusset, 21" (53.5 cm) long and 5¼" (13.5 cm) wide at widest point; handle enclosure, 6¾" (17 cm) long and 5" (12.5 cm) wide at widest point.

After felting: Bag, 4" (10 cm) wide at top, 9½" (24 cm) wide at widest point, 13¼" (33.5 cm) tall (excluding handle), 3¾" (9.5 cm) deep at base; handle enclosure, 5¾" (14.5 cm) long and 3½" (9 cm) wide.

yarn

Worsted weight (Medium #4).

Shown here: Manos del Uruguay Wool (100% wool; 138 yd [126 m]/100 g): #40 goldenrod (yellow) and #X topaz (orange), 1 skein each.

needles

U.S. size 11 (8 mm). Adjust needle size if necessary to obtain the correct gauge.

notions

Tapestry needle; 7–9" (18–23 cm) closed-bottom jeans zipper; 3" (7.5 cm) D-ring; four ⅜" (1 cm) Chicago screws; sewing needle and thread to match zipper; sewing pins; screwdriver; razor blade; pillowcase or lingerie bag with zipper.

gauge

13 sts and 18 rows = 4" (10 cm) in St st before felting; 18½ sts and 21 rows = 4" (10 cm) in St st after felting.

note

For the intarsia section, use separate lengths of yarn for each color section and twist the yarns together at color changes to avoid leaving holes. Wind each length of yarn into a small yarn butterfly or onto a bobbin to manage it easily.

Sunshine Chart

+	o	o	o	o	o	o	o	o	o	o	o	o	o	o	o	o	o	o	o	o	o	o	o	o	o	o	o	o	o	o	o	o	o	o	o	o	o	o	o	o	o	o	+
+	+	o	o	o	o	o	o	o	o	o	o	o	o	o	o	o	o	o	o	o	o	o	o	o	o	o	o	o	o	o	o	o	o	o	o	o	o	o	o	o	o	+	+	19
+	+	o	o	o	o	o	o	o	o	o	o	o	o	o	o	o	o	o	o	o	o	o	o	o	o	o	o	o	o	o	o	o	o	o	o	o	o	o	o	o	o	+	+
+	+	+	o	o	o	o	o	o	o	o	o	o	o	o	o	o	o	o	o	o	o	o	o	o	o	o	o	o	o	o	o	o	o	o	o	o	o	o	o	+	+	+	+	17
+	+	+	+	o	o	o	o	o	o	o	o	o	o	o	o	o	o	o	o	o	o	o	o	o	o	o	o	o	o	o	o	o	o	o	o	o	o	o	+	+	+	+	+
+	+	+	+	o	o	o	o	o	o	o	o	o	o	o	o	o	o	o	o	o	o	o	o	o	o	o	o	o	o	o	o	o	o	o	o	o	o	o	+	+	+	+	+	15
+	+	+	+	o	o	o	o	o	o	o	o	o	o	o	o	o	o	o	o	o	o	o	o	o	o	o	o	o	o	o	o	o	o	o	o	o	o	o	o	+	+	+	+
+	+	+	+	+	o	o	o	o	o	o	o	o	o	o	o	o	o	o	o	o	o	o	o	o	o	o	o	o	o	o	o	o	o	o	o	o	o	o	o	+	+	+	+	13
+	+	+	+	+	o	o	o	o	o	o	o	o	o	o	o	o	o	o	o	o	o	o	o	o	o	o	o	o	o	o	o	o	o	o	o	o	o	o	o	+	+	+	+
+	+	+	+	+	+	o	o	o	o	o	o	o	o	o	o	o	o	o	o	o	o	o	o	o	o	o	o	o	o	o	o	o	o	o	o	o	o	o	+	+	+	+	+	11
+	+	+	+	+	+	+	o	o	o	o	o	o	o	o	o	o	o	o	o	o	o	o	o	o	o	o	o	o	o	o	o	o	o	o	o	o	o	o	+	+	+	+	+
+	+	+	+	+	+	+	o	o	o	o	o	o	o	o	o	o	o	o	o	o	o	o	o	o	o	o	o	o	o	o	o	o	o	o	o	o	o	o	+	+	+	+	+	9
+	+	+	+	+	+	+	+	o	o	o	o	o	o	o	o	o	o	o	o	o	o	o	o	o	o	o	o	o	o	o	o	o	o	o	o	o	o	+	+	+	+	+	+
+	+	+	+	+	+	+	+	+	o	o	o	o	o	o	o	o	o	o	o	o	o	o	o	o	o	o	o	o	o	o	o	o	o	o	o	o	o	+	+	+	+	+	+	7
+	+	+	+	+	+	+	+	+	+	o	o	o	o	o	o	o	o	o	o	o	o	o	o	o	o	o	o	o	o	o	o	o	o	o	o	o	o	+	+	+	+	+	+
+	+	+	+	+	+	+	+	+	+	+	o	o	o	o	o	o	o	o	o	o	o	o	o	o	o	o	o	o	o	o	o	o	o	o	o	+	+	+	+	+	+	+	+	5
+	+	+	+	+	+	+	+	+	+	+	+	o	o	o	o	o	o	o	o	o	o	o	o	o	o	o	o	o	o	o	o	o	o	o	+	+	+	+	+	+	+	+	+
+	+	+	+	+	+	+	+	+	+	+	+	+	o	o	o	o	o	o	o	o	o	o	o	o	o	o	o	o	o	o	o	o	o	+	+	+	+	+	+	+	+	+	+	3
+	+	+	+	+	+	+	+	+	+	+	+	+	+	+	o	o	o	o	o	o	o	o	o	o	o	o	o	o	o	+	+	+	+	+	+	+	+	+	+	+	+	+	+
+	+	+	+	+	+	+	+	+	+	+	+	+	+	+	+	o	o	o	o	o	o	o	o	o	o	+	+	+	+	+	+	+	+	+	+	+	+	+	+	+	+	+	+	1

o	yellow
+	orange

BAG BACK

With orange, CO 26 sts.

Beg with a RS row, work 2 rows in St st.

Inc row: Using the knitted method (see Glossary, page 127), CO 2 sts at beg of row, work in St st to end—2 sts inc'd.

Rep inc row every row 5 more times—38 sts.

Next row: (RS) K1, k1f&b, knit to last 2 sts, k1f&b, k1—2 sts inc'd.

Next row: Purl.

Rep last 2 rows once more—42 sts.

Next row: CO 2 sts at beg of row, work according to Row 1 of Sunshine chart—44 sts.

Work Rows 2–20 of chart even.

D-ring handle

Chicago screws

Handle enclosure

Open for zipper

Gusset

decrease section

Row 1: (RS; dec row) K1, ssk, knit to last 3 sts, k2tog, k1—2 sts dec'd.

Rows 2–4: Work even in St st.

Rep Rows 1–4 five more times—32 sts rem.

Rep Rows 1–2 seven times—18 sts rem.

BO all sts.

BAG FRONT

Work as for bag back.

GUSSET

With orange, CO 3 sts.

Rows 1–4: Work in St st.

Row 5: (RS) K1f&b, k1, k1f&b—5 sts.

Rows 6–8: Work even in St st.

Row 9: K1, k1f&b, knit to last 2 sts, k1f&b, k1—2 sts inc'd.

Rep Rows 6–9 five more times—17 sts.

Work 37 rows even.

Next row: (RS) K1, ssk, knit to last 3 sts, k2tog, k1—2 sts dec'd.

Work 3 rows even in St st.

Rep last 4 rows 5 more times—5 sts rem.

Next row: Ssk, k1, k2tog—3 sts rem.

Work 3 rows even. BO all sts.

HANDLE ENCLOSURE
With yellow, CO 12 sts.

Rows 1 and 3: K1, k1f&b, knit to last 2 sts, k1f&b, k1—16 sts after Row 3.

Rows 2 and 4: Purl.

Work 24 rows even in St st.

Next row: K1, ssk, knit to last 3 sts, k2tog, k1—14 sts rem.

Next row: Purl.

Next row: (bind-off row) K1, ssk, pass knit st over ssk to BO 1 st, BO all sts to last 3 sts, k2tog, pass st over k2tog to BO 1 st, k1, pass k2tog over knit st to BO 1 st. Fasten off last st—no sts rem.

FINISHING
Pin one edge of gusset to CO edge of bag front, beg and ending at ends of orange section. Rep for bag back. Pin one side of bag front to bag back, leaving opposite side open for zipper. With orange threaded on a tapestry needle, sew gusset to bag front and back. With yellow threaded on a tapestry needle, sew bag side seam, then sew top of bag closed.

felt
Place pieces in pillowcase or lingerie bag. Wash on shortest, hottest cycle and lowest water level. (See page 21 for felting information.) Check pieces every 5 minutes for degree of felting. If necessary, stop the machine and reset to beginning of cycle; do not allow pieces to go through rinse or spin cycles. Remove from washer and shape to measurements. Allow to dry.

assembly
Sew in zipper (see right). Measure 1" (2.5 cm) diagonally in from each corner of handle enclosure piece and pierce using razor blade. Center handle enclosure piece on top of bag, folding equal amounts to front and back of bag. Pin in place. Slide screw through pierced hole and hold in place (see right).

On inside of bag, aligned with screw, pierce with razor blade and insert post. Secure screw into post. Repeat for other corner on same side. Unpin and slide handle enclosure through D-ring, then pin again. Insert and secure screws as for first side.

CHICAGO SCREWS & ZIPPERS

CHICAGO SCREWS

A lot of times I find hardware that sparks an idea that in turn will inspire an accessory. When that  happens, I rarely buy just one piece of the hardware; if I think I can do something with it, I'll buy it in whatever metals are available. Discovering Chicago screws was a moment that the world stopped, and all I could see were possibilities. You'll see the results in the Sunshine Intarsia Bag (page 30), the Half-Felted Bag (page 44), and the Big Brown Bag (page 80).

Chicago screws are made up of two pieces, a threaded screw and a post. The inside of the post is threaded to match the screw portion, so the pieces fit together smoothly and look like a miniature dumbbell. The head of the screw is slotted, while the end of the post is smooth.

Commonly used in leather work, Chicago screws hold thick leather pieces together securely without sewing them. They can be incredibly useful when attaching a different kind of handle to your felted bag. They are used to secure the handles of the three bags.

To insert a Chicago screw, begin by using a razor blade to pierce the felt where the screw will be inserted. (It may help to enlarge the hole with an awl, screwdriver, or the hole cutter from a grommet set kit.) Slide the screw portion into the hole and hold it in place, then insert the post on the reverse of the fabric. (Be careful not to make the hole too large; felted knit fabric stretches.) Use your fingers to screw the pieces together and tighten with the flat-head screwdriver.

Be very careful when using the razor blade. Keep your fingers clear of the blade and put it away after use.

ZIPPERS

Sewing in a zipper can be tricky, but it creates a clean look and a secure closure. Inserting a zipper in a closed space like the inside of a bag requires a few extra steps to conceal the stitches and make sure the zipper is even.

With right side of bag facing and zipper closed, pin zipper to edges of bag so edges almost cover the zipper teeth. Tuck the ends of the zipper inside the piece. If the zipper is a bit too long, line up the top teeth with the top of the opening, and pin the zipper at the bottom of the opening. With thread to match bag and right side facing, use a running stitch to baste zipper in place close to teeth. Open zipper, turn piece inside out, and close zipper nearly to top. (It will be easier to sew the zipper in neatly if it's closed, but you may need to leave it open a bit so that you can turn the piece right side out again.) With wrong sides facing and using matching thread, stitch outer edges of zipper to wrong side of bag. Sew into the fabric of the piece, but do not pass the needle to the outside to keep the stitches hidden. Stitch zipper again with matching thread, this time as close as possible to the edges of the bag opening, including the top and bottom edges. Open the zipper and turn the piece right side out. Check that the zipper appears even and opens easily, then remove the basting stitches.

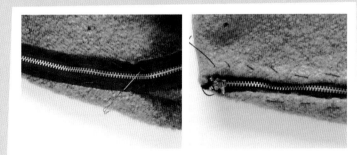

ſIDE ſLIP CLOCHE

I don't use many novelty yarns, but the subtle sparkle in this blend makes it one of my favorites. Knitted tightly, it looks like woven fabric. Stitches are increased on one side to make the hat slouch. This is designed to be worn with the wrong side of the ruffles facing forward.

finished size
20½" (52 cm) circumference. To fit 22" (56 cm) head circumference.

yarn
Worsted weight (Medium #4).
Shown here: Rowan RYC Soft Lux (64% merino, 10% angora, 24% nylon, 2% metallic fiber; 137 yd [125 m]/50 g): #011 camel, 2 skeins.

needles
U.S. size 5 (3.75 mm): 16" (40 cm) circular (cir) and set of 4 or 5 double-pointed (dpn). Adjust needle size if necessary to obtain the correct gauge.

notions
Small stitch holder; 4 locking-ring stitch markers; markers (m); tapestry needle.

gauge
20 sts and 32 rows = 4" (10 cm) in St st; 23 sts and 32 rows = 4" (10 cm) in rib patt.

construction
The hat is made in three pieces: a large ruffle and a small ruffle are knitted separately, then joined and continued to form the band. Stitches are picked up along the band and joined in the round to work the hat.

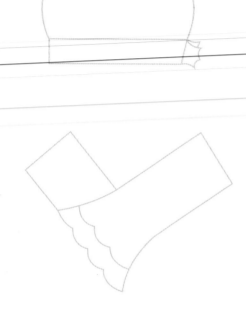

HAT

large ruffle

CO 32 sts. Do not join.

Row 1: (RS) [K7, p1] 4 times.
Row 2: [K1, p7] 4 times.
Row 3: [K5, k2tog, p1] 4 times—28 sts rem.
Rows 4, 6, and 8: Work in rib patt as
   established (working sts as they appear).
Row 5: [K4, k2tog, p1] 4 times—24 sts rem.
Row 7: [K3, k2tog, p1] 4 times—20 sts rem.
Row 9: [K2, k2tog, p1] 4 times—16 sts rem.
Row 10: Work in rib patt as established.

Place sts onto holder.

small ruffle

CO 24 sts. Do not join.

Row 1: (RS) [K5, p1] 4 times.
Rows 2 and 4: Work in rib patt as established.
Row 3: [K3, k2tog, p1] 4 times—20 sts rem.
Row 5: [K2, k2tog, p1] 4 times—16 sts rem.
Row 6: Work in rib patt as established.

Place large ruffle sts onto a dpn and hold
behind small ruffle, with RS of large ruffle
facing WS of small ruffle.

Next row: [Work 1 st from left needle tog with 1
   st from dpn in patt] 16 times.
Next row: [K1, p3] 4 times.

band

Cont in rib as established until piece measures
20½" (52 cm) from large ruffle CO, ending
with a WS row. BO all sts in rib patt.

join end of band to ruffles

Pin BO edge of band to left edge of large ruffle. With yarn threaded on a tapestry needle, use mattress st (see Glossary, page 131) to sew pieces together as shown. Block band.

body

Beg at BO edge of band on the opposite end from the CO of large ruffle, use 4 locking markers to divide the selvedge edge of band into four equal parts. Using markers as a guide and beg at BO edge of band, pick up and knit 96 sts evenly spaced along edge of band. Place marker (pm) and join for working in the rnd.

Rnd 1: Knit.

Rnd 2: (inc rnd) [K2, M1 (see Glossary, page 129)] 11 times, k51, [k2, M1] 11 times, k1—118 sts.

Work in St st until piece measures 4¼" (11 cm) from pick-up rnd.

Next rnd: (dec rnd) [K27, k2tog] 4 times, k2—114 sts rem.

Next rnd: [K2tog, k15, ssk, pm] 6 times—102 sts rem.

Next rnd: Knit.

Next rnd: [K2tog, knit to 2 sts before m, ssk] 6 times—12 sts dec'd.

Rep last 2 rnds 6 more times—18 sts rem.

Next rnd: K2tog 9 times—9 sts rem.

Next rnd: K2tog 4 times, k1—5 sts rem.

Pull tail through rem sts and fasten off inside. Weave in loose ends.

ALPACA SILK BOW SCARF

I love to see how women style their scarves. This scarf was made specifically to be tied in a bow, which is always one of my favorite ways to see one worn. The detailed but unfussy intarsia patterning shows at the ends. The ribbing stops at the bows, giving the illusion of shaping without the work.

finished size
9½' (2.9 m) long, 4" (10 cm) wide in ribbed sections, and 6¼" (16 cm) wide at widest point.

yarn
DK weight (Light #3).
Shown here: Blue Sky Alpacas Alpaca Silk (50% alpaca, 50% silk; 146 yd [134 m]/50 g): #128 plum (dark purple), 4 skeins, and #129 amethyst (light purple), 1 skein.

needles
U.S. size 5 (3.75 mm). Adjust needle size if necessary to obtain the correct gauge.

notions
3 bobbins; tapestry needle.

gauge
22 sts and 28 rows = 4" (10 cm) in St st; 39 sts and 28 rows = 4" (10 cm) in rib patt.

construction
The scarf is worked in intarsia to create the vertical crossed stripe, switching from rib to stockinette stitch for the wide bow. For the intarsia section, use separate lengths of yarn for each color section and twist the yarns together at color changes to avoid leaving holes. Wind each length of yarn into a small yarn butterfly or onto a bobbin to manage it easily.

Intarsia Chart

39
37
35
33
31
29
27
25
23
21
19
17
15
13
11
9
7
5
3
1

■ with dark purple, k on RS; p on WS

▨ with dark purple, p on RS; k on WS

◺ with light purple, k on RS; p on WS

▫ with light purple, p on RS; k on WS

SCARF

CO 17 sts with dark purple, CO 5 sts with light purple, CO 17 sts with dark purple—39 sts total.

first rib section

Setup row: (RS) With dark purple, [k1, p1] 8 times, k1, with light purple, [k1, p1] 2 times, k1, with dark purple, [k1, p1] 8 times, k1. Work in color and rib patt as established (working sts as they appear) until piece measures 7" (18 cm), ending with a WS row.

first chart section

Work Rows 1–40 of Intarsia chart.

second rib section

Work even in color and rib patt (as for first rib section) until second rib section measures 8" (20.5 cm), ending with a WS row.

first bow

Next row: With dark purple, k1, p1, k1, p1, k13, with light purple, k5, with dark purple, knit to last 4 sts, p1, k1, p1, k1.

Working sts as they appear and maintaining colors as established, work even until bow section measures 12½" (31.5 cm), ending with a WS row.

center section

Next row: With dark purple, [k1, p1] 8 times, k1, with light purple, [k1, p1] 2 times, k1, with dark purple, [k1, p1] 8 times, k1.

Cont in color and rib patt as established until center section measures 47" (119.5 cm), ending with a WS row.

second bow

Work as for first bow.

third rib section

Work as for second rib section.

second chart section

Work Rows 1–40 of Intarsia chart.

fourth rib section

Work as for first rib section. BO all sts.

FINISHING

Weave in loose ends, working ends into corresponding color sections.

HALF-FELTED BAG

I love the look of mixing felted and unfelted knits, but this time the technique is practical, too. Load up on adornment: chain handle, Chicago screws, soft leather lacing, cord lock stops, D-rings, and sew-on magnets. Get out your tools!

finished size
19" (48.5 cm) wide and 21½" (54.5 cm) tall before felting; 13½" (34.5 cm) wide and 12" (30.5 cm) tall after felting.

yarn
Worsted weight (Medium #4).
Shown here: Brown Sheep Lamb's Pride Worsted (85% wool, 15% mohair; 190 yd [174 m]/4 oz): M-176 silver gray, 3 skeins.

needles
U.S. size 11 (8 mm), U.S. size 7 (4.5 mm), and U.S. size 6 (4 mm): 16" (40 cm) circular (cir). Adjust needle size if necessary to obtain the correct gauge.

notions
4 markers (1 in a contrasting color); 24" (61 cm) heavy chain; four ¾" (2 cm) nickel Chicago screws; two ¾" (2 cm) D-rings; 2 cord lock stops; 2 sew-on magnetic snaps; sewing needle and thread; sewing pins; 60" (152.5 cm) gray deer-leather lacing, cut into four equal lengths; pillowcase or lingerie bag with zipper; 2 sets needle-nose pliers; flat-head screwdriver; razor blade.

gauge
13½ sts and 17½ rows = 4" (10 cm) in St st on largest needles before felting; 19 sts and 31 rows = 4" (10 cm) in St st on largest needles after felting; 24 sts and 26 rows = 4" (10 cm) in k3, p1 rib on smallest needles.

construction
Knit the front and back, two pockets, and ring holders separately. Felt the front, back, and ring holders, then assemble the bag and add hardware.

BAG BACK
With largest needles, CO 42 sts.

Work 2 rows in St st.

Cont in St st, use the knitted method (see Glossary, page 127) to CO 2 sts at beg of next 6 rows—54 sts.

Inc row: (RS) K1, k1f&b, knit to last 2 sts, k1f&b, k1—2 sts inc'd.

Purl 1 row.
Rep inc row—58 sts.
Work 3 rows even in St st.
Rep last 4 rows 3 more times—64 sts.

shape pocket
BO 10 sts at beg of next 2 rows—44 sts rem.
BO 1 st at beg of next 2 rows—42 sts rem.
BO 3 sts at beg of next 2 rows—36 sts rem.
BO 2 sts at beg of next 2 rows—32 sts rem.
BO 1 st at beg of next 4 rows—28 sts rem.

Work 8 rows even in St st.

Next row: (RS) K1, k1f&b, knit to last 2 sts, k1f&b, k1—2 sts inc'd.
Next row: Purl.

Rep last 2 rows 5 more times—40 sts.
CO 3 sts at beg of next 2 rows—46 sts.
CO 8 sts at beg of next 2 rows—62 sts.
Work 2 rows even in St st.

Next row: (RS) K1, ssk, knit to last 3 sts, k2tog, k1—2 sts dec'd.
Next row: Purl.

Rep last 2 rows 9 more times—42 sts rem.

BO 8 sts at beg of next 2 rows—26 sts rem.

Work 8 rows even. BO all sts.

BAG FRONT
Work as for Bag Back.

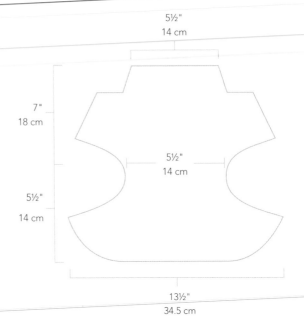

5½"
14 cm

7"
18 cm

5½"
14 cm

5½"
14 cm

13½"
34.5 cm

FELTED RING HOLDERS
(make 2)

With largest needles, CO 6 sts.

Row 1: K1, k1f&b, knit to last 2 sts, k1f&b, k1—2 sts inc'd.

Row 2: Purl.

Rep Rows 1 and 2 once more—10 sts.

Work even in St st for 12 rows.

Next row: K1, ssk, knit to last 3 sts, k2tog, k1—2 sts dec'd.

Next row: Purl.

Rep last 2 rows once more—6 sts rem. Work 10 rows in St st. BO all sts.

UNFELTED POCKETS
(make 2)

With middle-size needles, CO 102 sts. Place marker (pm) in contrasting color to indicate beg of rnd. Join for working in the rnd, being careful not to twist sts.

Rnd 1: Knit.

Rnd 2: K1, pm, k50, pm, k1, pm, k50.

Rnd 3: (dec rnd) K1, ssk, knit to 2 sts before m, k2tog, sl m, k1, sl m, ssk, knit to last 2 sts, k2tog—4 sts dec'd.

Rep Rnd 3 every rnd 5 more times—78 sts rem.

ribbed section

Change to smallest needles.

Next rnd: K1, remove m, k2tog, k1, p1, *k3, p1; rep from * to 2 sts before m, k2, ssk, removing markers, p1, *k3, p1; rep from * to end of rnd—76 sts rem.

Next rnd: *K3, p1; rep from * to end of rnd.

Rep last rnd 17 more times.

Next rnd: (eyelet rnd) *Yo, k2tog, k1, p1; rep from * to end of rnd.

Work next 6 rnds in rib patt as established. BO all sts in patt.

FINISHING

With yarn threaded on a tapestry needle and WS tog, sew sides of front and back, leaving top and side pockets open. Weave in loose ends.

felting

Place bag and ring holders in pillowcase or lingerie bag. Wash on shortest, hottest cycle and lowest water level. (See page 21 for information on felting.) Check pieces for degree of felting every 5 minutes; if necessary, reset the washing machine to begin again, but do not allow the pieces to go through a rinse or spin cycle. When they are sufficiently felted, remove the pieces from the washer and shape to measurements. If necessary, use razor blade to open sides of ring holders. Allow to dry completely.

attach pockets

With WS of pocket and RS of bag held tog, line up pocket side decreases with top and bottom of bag's pocket opening. Pull pocket 2½" (6.5 cm) over top of pocket opening and secure with pins. Pull pocket 2¾" (7 cm) over bottom of pocket opening and secure with pins. Match center of pocket opening to center of pocket, pull pocket over ¾" (2 cm), and pin. Pin remainder of pocket in place around opening. With sewing needle and thread, backstitch (see Glossary, page 130) pocket in place. Rep for second side and pocket.

insert lacing

With 2 strands of lacing threaded on a tapestry needle and beg 5 eyelets from top, pull leather in and out of all eyelets around entire pocket, ending at beginning eyelet, so all ends of leather lacing are coming out of same eyelet. Take care not to twist leather too much through eyelets.

Hold all 4 leather ends together and pass through cord lock, leaving 3½" (9 cm) tails. Trim ends even.

Hardware attached to bag

attaching hardware

Grasp the D-ring near the opening with 1 set of pliers and use the second pair to twist the ring open just enough to pass one length of chain through and twist ring closed. Rep for other end of chain.

Slide smaller end of one felted ring holder through D-ring. On top side seam of bag, place smaller end of felted ring holder inside bag, fold larger end over outside of bag, and secure with sewing pins. Measure 1" (2.5 cm) from top of folded ring holder. Using razor blade, carefully pierce all 3 layers. Pass Chicago screw through hole from inside to outside and attach other end, tightening with a screwdriver if necessary. Repeat to insert a second screw through only the felted bag and ring holder ¾" (2 cm) below the first. Repeat to attach D-rings and chain to other side of bag. With sewing needle and thread, sew magnet snaps to each side of bag opening.

WORKING WITH CHAIN & D-RINGS

Chains, D-rings, and jump rings all work like complete enclosed pieces of metal most of the time, but they have separations where they can be opened to link other items together. It may seem like the easiest way of opening them is just pulling the sides apart, but it is just about impossible to bend the links back into their original shape, and whatever you're trying to hold together will most likely come apart.

Instead of pulling them apart, the best way to open these links is to use a little bit of torque. Locate the opening and hold each side with a separate set of pliers. (If the jaws of the pliers are serrated or rough, wrap them in a few layers of tape to protect the metal.) Use the pliers to pull one side of opening toward you while holding the other side steady. Open the link just enough to slip on the items you need to hold. Then reverse the direction, pulling the sides together to meet seamlessly.

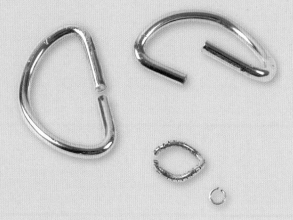

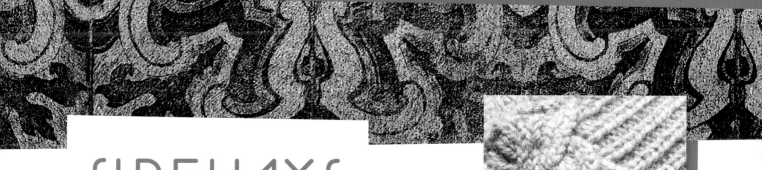

SIDEWAYS GRANDE HAT

Welcome the bitterest winters in this oversize hat. This ribbed cloche-shaped cap, worked in warm alpaca, is finished with a twisted faux cable that runs from brim to crown. Wear the cable off center or at the side of the head.

finished size
20" (51 cm) circumference. To fit 21½–23" (54.5–58.5 cm) head circumference.

yarn
Chunky weight (Bulky #5).
Shown here: Plymouth Baby Alpaca Grande (100% baby alpaca; 110 yd [101 m]/100 g): #401 gray, 2 skeins.

needles
U.S. size 7 (4.5 mm), U.S. size 8 (5 mm), U.S. size 9 (5.5 mm), and U.S. size 10 (6 mm). Adjust needle size if necessary to obtain the correct gauge.

notions
2 locking-ring markers; tapestry needle.

gauge
22½ sts and 20 rows = 4" (10 cm) in rib patt on largest needles.

construction
The hat is knitted from side to side in one piece, then stitches are picked up for the crown and cable.

HAT

brim

With largest needles, CO 42 sts.

Row 1: (WS) *K2, p1; rep from * to last 3 sts, k3.
Row 2: Work sts as they appear.
Rep Rows 1 and 2 until piece measures 14½" (37 cm) from CO.

Change to second largest needles and continue in patt until piece measures 16" (40.5 cm) from CO.

Change to second smallest needles and continue in patt until piece measures 17½" (44.5 cm) from CO.

Change to smallest needles and continue in patt until piece measures 20" (51 cm) from CO.

BO all sts in patt.

crown

With second largest needles, RS facing, and beg at CO edge, pick up and knit 68 sts along selvedge to BO edge.

Rows 1, 3, 5, 7, and 9: (WS) Purl.
Row 2: (dec row) K1, *k4, k2tog; rep from * to last st, k1—57 sts rem.
Row 4: K1, *k3, k2tog; rep from * to last st, k1—46 sts rem.
Row 6: K1, *k2, k2tog; rep from * to last st, k1—35 sts rem.
Row 8: K1, *k1, k2tog; rep from * to last st, k1—24 sts rem.
Row 10: K1, *k2tog; rep from * to last st, k1—13 sts rem.
Row 11: P1, *p2tog; rep from * to last 2 sts, p2—8 sts rem.

Cut yarn, leaving an 8" (20.5 cm) tail. Pull tail through rem 8 sts and fasten off inside.

With yarn threaded on a tapestry needle, use mattress st (see Glossary, page 131) to sew side of hat, being sure to line up ribs.

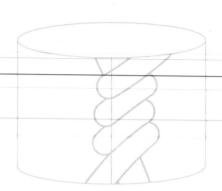

cable

first strap

At bottom edge of hat, measure 1" (2.5 cm) on each side of seam. Mark with locking-ring markers.

With WS facing and largest needles, pick up and knit 4 sts between m and seam on each side of m—8 sts total.

Row 1: (RS of hat; WS of strap) K2, p1, k2, p1, k2.
Row 2: P2, k1, p2, k1, p2.
Rep Rows 1 and 2 until piece measures 7¼" (18.5 cm) from picked up edge, ending with Row 1.

Next row: (bind-off row) P1, p2tog, pass purl st over p2tog to BO 1 st, BO all sts to last 3 sts, p2tog, pass st over p2tog to BO 1 st, p1, pass p2tog over purl st to BO 1 st. Fasten off last st—no sts rem.

second strap

With WS facing, measure 2" (5 cm) to the right of first cable strap and mark with locking-ring marker. With WS facing and largest needles, pick up and knit 8 sts between marker and first strap.

Beg with Row 1, work as for first strap.

FINISHING

Wrap the two straps around each other 3 times, being sure that they lie flat against hat. With yarn threaded on a tapestry needle, sew BO edges of straps to last horizontal rib of hat near crown. Use running st (see Glossary, page 131) to secure cable to hat. Weave in loose ends.

RAGLAN WRAP

This is a garment best suited for layering. The large raglan sleeves are cut a bit short. A high neck and asymmetrical faux button band hide large hidden snaps for closure. This wrap will become a standard in your wardrobe.

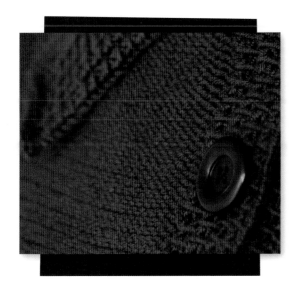

finished size
31½ (38, 43½)" (80 [96.5, 110.5] cm) bust circumference. Wrap shown measures 31½" (80 cm).

yarn
DK weight (Light #3). *Shown here:* Rowan Wool Cotton (50% merino, 50% cotton; 124 yd [113 m]/50 g): #910 gypsy, 9 (13, 16) balls.

needles
U.S. sizes 6 (4 mm) and 7 (4.5 mm). Adjust needle size if necessary to obtain the correct gauge.

notions
Tapestry needle; six 1⅛" (3 cm) buttons; 6 size 4 sew-on snaps (see Sources, page 134); sewing needle and matching thread.

gauge
22 sts and 30 rows = 4" (10 cm) in rev St st on smaller needles.

construction
The fronts, sleeves, and back of the piece are worked separately and sewn together, with stitches picked up for the collar.

BACK

With smaller needles, CO 86 (104, 120) sts.

Row 1: (RS) K2, *yo, k2, pass yo over last 2 sts; rep from * to last 2 sts, k2.

Row 2: Purl.

Rep Rows 1 and 2 nine more times.

Next row: (RS) K1, purl to last st, k1.

Next row: P1, knit to last st, p1.

Rep last 2 rows 6 (10, 14) more times.

shape raglan

Row 1: (dec row) K1, yo, k2, pass yo over last 2 sts, ssk, purl to last 5 sts, k2tog, yo, k2, pass yo over last 2 sts, k1—2 sts dec'd.

Row 2: P4, knit to last 4 sts, p4.

Row 3: K1, yo, k2, pass yo over last 2 sts, k1, purl to last 4 sts, k1, yo, k2, pass yo over last 2 sts, k1.

Row 4: P4, knit to last 4 sts, p4.

Rep last 4 rows 23 (19, 14) more times, then rep Rows 1 and 2 one (twelve, twenty-four) time(s)—36 (40, 42) sts rem. BO all sts.

RIGHT FRONT

With smaller needles, CO 61 (71, 81) sts.

Row 1: (RS) K1, *yo, k2, pass yo over last 2 sts; rep from * to last 2 sts, k2.

Row 2: Purl.

Rep Rows 1 and 2 nine more times.

Next row: (RS) K1, *yo, k2, pass yo over last 2 sts; rep from * 3 more times, purl to last st, k1.

Next row: P1, knit to last 9 sts, p9.

Rep last 2 rows 6 (10, 14) more times.

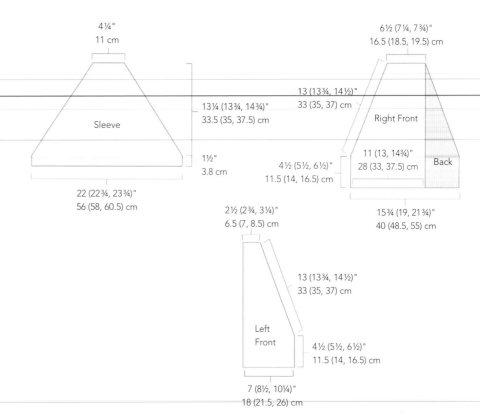

shape raglan

Row 1: (dec row) K1, *yo, k2, pass yo over last 2 sts; rep from * 3 more times, purl to last 5 sts, k2tog, yo, k2, pass yo over last 2 sts, k1—1 st dec'd.

Row 2: P4, knit to last 9 sts, p9.

Row 3: K1, *yo, k2, pass yo over last 2 sts; rep from * 3 more times, purl to last 4 sts, k1, yo, k2, pass yo over last 2 sts, k1.

Row 4: P4, knit to last 9 sts, p9.

Rep last 4 rows 23 (19, 14) more times, then rep Rows 1 and 2 one (twelve, twenty-four) time(s)—36 (39, 42) sts rem.

BO all sts.

LEFT FRONT

With smaller needles, CO 39 (47, 57) sts.

Row 1: K2, *yo, k2, pass yo over last 2 sts; rep from * to last st, k1.

Row 2: Purl.

Rep Rows 1 and 2 nine more times.

Next row: (RS) K1, purl to last 9 sts, *yo, k2, pass yo over last 2 sts; rep from * 3 more times, k1.

Next row: P9, knit to last st, p1.

Rep last 2 rows 6 (10, 14) more times.

shape raglan

Row 1: (dec row) K1, yo, k2, pass yo over last 2 sts, ssk, purl to last 9 sts, *yo, k2, pass yo over last 2 sts; rep from * 3 more times, k1—1 st dec'd.

Row 2: P9, knit to last 4 sts, p4.

Row 3: K1, yo, k2, pass yo over last 2 sts, k1, purl to last 9 sts, *yo, k2, pass yo over last 2 sts; rep from * 3 more times, k1.

Row 4: P9, knit to last 4 sts, p4.

Rep last 4 rows 23 (19, 14) more times, then rep Rows 1 and 2 one (twelve, twenty-four) time(s)—14 (15, 18) sts rem.

BO all sts.

SLEEVES

With larger needles, CO 124 (128, 134) sts.

Row 1: (RS) K2, *yo, k2, pass yo over last 2 sts; rep from * to last 2 sts, k2.

Row 2: Purl.

Rep Rows 1 and 2 four more times.

shape raglan

Change to smaller needles.

Row 1: (dec row) K1, ssk, purl to last 3 sts, k2tog, k1—2 sts dec'd.

Row 2: P2, knit to last 2 sts, p2.

Rep last 2 rows 49 (51, 54) more times—24 sts rem.

BO all sts.

FINISHING

Block pieces. With yarn threaded on a tapestry needle, use mattress st (see Glossary, page 131) to sew sleeves to back, sew fronts to sleeves, and sew side and sleeve seams.

collar

With RS facing and smaller needles, beg at center front, pick up and knit 36 (39, 42) sts along right front neck, 21 sts along sleeve, 36 (40, 42) sts along back neck, 21 sts along sleeve, and 14 (15, 18) sts along left front neck—128 (136, 144) sts total.

Row 1: (RS of collar; WS of wrap) K1, *yo, k2, pass yo over last 2 sts; rep from * 3 more times, [k2, p2] 27 (29, 31) times, k2, *yo, k2, pass yo over last 2 sts; rep from * 3 more times, k1.

Row 2: P11, [k2, p2] 27 (29, 31) times, p9.

Rep Rows 1 and 2 until collar measures 8" (20.5 cm), ending with Row 2. BO all sts in patt. Weave in loose ends.

buttons and snaps

With RS of right front facing, use needle and thread to sew 1 button 1½" (3.8 cm) from CO edge at center of button band. Sew 1 button 1½" (3.8 cm) above beg of collar portion at center of button band. Sew rem 4 buttons evenly spaced between top and bottom buttons.

Sew pronged portions of snaps directly behind buttons on WS of right front. Mark snap position on RS of left button band, then sew recessed portion of snap to RS of left front to correspond with first portion.

Sew snaps behind buttons.

ARGYLE LACE HAT

This tam is like a box of miniature pastries, filled with small bites of sweet things, beginning with a fancy rib stitch and continuing with just a little bit of lace. Choose a feminine or cheeky fabric to cover the buttons for the finishing touch.

finished size
16¼" (41.5 cm) circumference at brim, unstretched. To fit 21–22" (53.5–56 cm) head circumference.

yarn
Sportweight (Fine #2).
Shown here: Blue Sky Alpacas Sport Weight (100% alpaca; 110 yd [101 m]/50 g): #500 natural white, 2 skeins.

needles
U.S. size 2½ (3 mm). U.S. size 4 (3.5 mm): 16" (40 cm) circular (cir) and set of 4 or 5 double-pointed (dpn). Adjust needle size if necessary to obtain the correct gauge.

notions
Markers (m); seven ⅝" (1.5 cm) half-ball covered buttons; ⅛ yd (11.5 cm) cotton fabric; sewing needle and matching thread.

gauge
26 sts and 34 rows = 4" (10 cm) in St st on larger needles.

construction
Begin the hat by working back and forth through the end of the lace pattern, then join for working in the round to complete the shaping.

stitch guide

Make bobble (MB): (Knit into front, back, front, back) of same st (4 new sts on right needle), pass first 3 sts over last st on right needle—I st rem.

	k on RS; p on WS
·	p on RS; k on WS
O	yo
╱	k2tog
╲	ssk
⋏	sl 1, k2tog, psso
●	MB (see Stitch Guide)
▢	pattern repeat

Argyle Chart

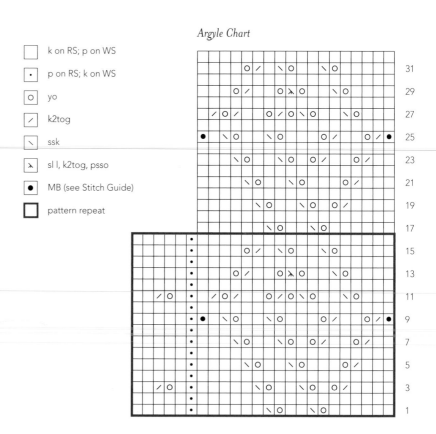

HAT

brim

With smaller cir needle, CO 125 sts. Do not join.

Row 1: (RS) K2, p1, k6, *p3, k1, p3, k3; rep from * 10 more times, p1, k5.

Row 2: P5, k1, p3, *k3, p1, k3, p3; rep from * 10 more times, p3, k1, p2.

Row 3: (buttonhole row) K2, p1, k6, *p3, k1, p3, k3; rep from * 10 more times, p1, k1, yo, k2tog, k2.

Row 4: P5, k1, p3, knit to last 6 sts, p3, k1, p2.

Rep Rows 1 and 2, then Rows 1 and 4, then Rows 1–4—8 rows total. Rep last 8 rows once more, then rep Rows 1 and 2.

increase section

Change to larger needle.

Row 1: (RS; inc row) K2, p1, k7, [M1, k2] 52 times, k5, p1, k5—177 sts.

Row 2: P5, k1, p18, pm, purl to last 3 sts, k1, p2.

argyle lace

Row 1: K2, p1, knit to m, work Row 1 of Argyle chart.

Row 2: Work Row 2 of chart, purl to last 3 sts, k1, p2.

Cont as established through Row 16 of chart. Rep Rows 1–16 once more.

crown

Rnd 1: K2, p1, k3, ssk, k70, k2tog, k71, k2tog, work Row 17 of chart, place marker (pm) for beginning of rnd—174 sts rem; 6 sts left at end of row, to be worked at beg of next row.

Rnd 2: Sl last 6 sts of previous row to dpn and hold in front of next 6 sts on left needle, purl 1 st from left needle tog with 1 st from dpn, [knit 1 st from dpn tog with 1 st from left needle] 5 times, k19, pm, *k25, pm; rep from * 4 more times, work Row 18 of chart—168 sts rem.

Rnds 3, 5, 7, 9, 11, 13, and 15: *Ssk, knit to 2 sts before m, k2tog,; rep from * 5 more times, work next odd row of chart—84 sts rem after Rnd 15.

Rnds 4, 6, 8, 10, 12, and 14: Knit.

Rnd 16: *Ssk, knit to 2 sts before m, k2tog; rep from * 6 more times—14 sts dec'd.

Rnds 17–19: Rep Rnd 16 three more times—28 sts rem after Rnd 19.

Rnd 20: *K1, k2tog; rep from * 8 more times, k1—20 sts rem.

Rnd 21: *K2tog; rep from * 9 more times—10 sts rem.

Cut yarn, draw tail through remaining sts, and fasten off inside.

FINISHING

Weave in loose ends and block lightly. Cover buttons with fabric (see opposite). With needle and thread, sew buttons to correspond with buttonholes.

CUSTOM BUTTONS

It takes a little extra effort, but creating the perfect buttons to complete your piece can give it a unique and polished finish. I used a plaid fabric on the buttons of the Argyle Lace Hat to add some color and continue the Scottish theme.

The button kit package will probably give instructions for completing the buttons. Cut the fabric in circles following the pattern for your selected buttons and center the fabric wrong side up over the mold. Hold the fabric firmly and press the button shell into the mold. Tuck the fabric into the button shell, then place the back over the tucked fabric. Press down firmly with the pusher to snap the parts of the button into place.

A panel of continuous color changes, both stranded and intarsia, creates a distinct and modern look in these fingerless mitts. A seed-stitch wristband fastened with a leather button completes the look.

TEAK BITTERSWEET GAUNTLETS

finished size
8½" (21.5 cm) long, 7½" (19 cm) hand circumference, 5¾" (14.5 cm) wrist circumference. To fit a woman's size small to medium.

yarn
Fingering weight (Super fine #1).
Shown here: Rowan 4-ply Soft (100% merino wool; 191 yd [175 m]/50 g): brown mittens, #397 teak (brown; MC) and #396 clover (mauve; CC), 1 ball each; mauve mittens, #396 clover (mauve; MC) and #397 teak (brown; CC), 1 ball each.

needles
U.S. size 2 (2.75 mm) and U.S. size 1 (2.25 mm). Adjust needle size if necessary to obtain the correct gauge.

notions
2 markers (m); sewing needle and matching thread; four ⅝" (1.6 cm) leather buttons; tapestry needle.

gauge
30 sts and 42 rows = 4" (10 cm) in St st on larger needles; 32 sts and 32 rows = 4" (10 cm) in charted patt on larger needles.

construction
The mitts are worked flat, following the chart for the color panels. The button straps are knitted separately.

stitch guide

Bobble: (K1, p1, k1) into same st, turn; p3, turn; sl 1, k2tog, psso.

LEFT HAND

cuff

With larger needles and MC, CO 71 sts.

Row 1: (RS) K35, place marker (pm), k1, pm, k35.

Rows 2–4: Work in St st, slipping markers as you come to them.

Row 5: K1, ssk, knit to 2 sts before m, k2tog, k1, ssk, knit to last 3 sts, k2tog, k1—4 sts dec'd.

Rows 6–8: Work even in St st.

Rep Rows 5–8 six more times—43 sts rem.

Remove markers.

Work 8 rows even in St st.

Hand Chart

with MC, k on RS, p on WS

with MC, p on RS, k on WS

with CC, k on RS, p on WS

with MC, make bobble (see Stitch Guide)

pattern repeat

thumb gusset

Row 1: (RS; inc row) K1, k1f&b, knit to last 2 sts, k1f&b, k1—2 sts inc'd.

Row 2: Purl.

Rep Rows 1 and 2 four more times—53 sts.

Work 2 rows even in St st.

[Rep Rows 1 and 2, then work even in St st for 2 rows] 2 times—57 sts.

With MC, k1, M1 (see Glossary, page 129), k4, pm, work 21 sts according to Hand chart, pm, knit to end of row—58 sts.

Cont as established, working Hand chart Rows 2–4 between m, then working Hand chart Rows 1–4 between m 5 more times, and working sts outside m in St st.

Change to smaller needles. Work Hand chart Rows 5–8 between m, working sts outside m in St st. BO all sts.

RIGHT HAND

Work as for left hand to start of chart.

With MC, k31, pm, work 21 sts according to Hand chart, pm, k4, M1, k1—58 sts.

Cont as established, working Hand chart Rows 2–4 between m, then working Hand chart Rows 1–4 between m 5 more times, and working sts outside m in St st.

Change to smaller needles. Work Hand chart Rows 5–8 between m, working sts outside m in St st. BO all sts.

STRAP (make 2)

With MC and larger needles, CO 5 sts.

Row 1: K1f&b, k1, p1, k1f&b, k1—7 sts.

Rows 2–13: *K1, p1; rep from * to last st, k1.

Row 14: (buttonhole row) K1, p1, k1, yo, k2tog, p1, k1.

Rows 15–31: *K1, p1; rep from * to last st, k1.

Rep buttonhole row.

Work 67 more rows in patt.

Next row: (bind-off row) K1, ssk, pass knit st over ssk to BO 1 st, p1, pass ssk over purl st to BO 1 st, k2tog, pass purl st over k2tog to BO 1 st, k1, pass k2tog over knit st to BO 1 st. Fasten off last st—no sts rem.

FINISHING

Block lightly. With MC threaded on a tapestry needle, use mattress stitch (see Glossary, page 131) to sew sides of each mitt from CO edge up 4½" (11.5 cm) and from BO edge down 2½" (6.5 cm), leaving 1½" (3.8 cm) open for thumb.

strap

With sewing needle and thread, sew one button to RS of plain end of strap. Pull button through second buttonhole. Sew second button to strap to correspond with remaining buttonhole. Weave in loose ends.

HOODIE DEVOTED

We've all been converted—who doesn't put on a hoodie for warmth and comfort? I wanted to create a hoodie to accessorize my outfit, not dominate it—to fit under a coat or over a dress. This lined hood achieves both practicality and style: cozy to keep out the breezes, stunning worn on its own.

finished size
18¾" (47.5 cm) tall at front of hood, 14½" (37 cm) tall at back of hood, and 13" (33 cm) deep, excluding ribbing.

yarn
Worsted weight (Medium #4).
Shown here: Vermont Organic Fiber Co. O-Wool Classic (100% organic merino; 198 yd [181 m]/100 g): #6402 saffron, 4 skeins.

needles
U.S. size 8 (5 mm): 24" (60 cm) circular (cir) and set of 2 double-pointed (dpn). U.S. size 9 (5.5 mm): 24" (60 cm) cir.

notions
Cable needle (cn); large stitch holder; marker (m); locking-ring marker; pins; two 1⅛" (2.9 cm) wood beads; 2" (5 cm) piece of cardboard; 1 yd (1 m) cotton fabric; sewing needle and thread; tapestry needle; sewing machine (optional).

gauge
23 sts and 27 rows = 4" (10 cm) in cable patt on larger needle.
20 sts and 22 rows = 4" (10 cm) in rib patt on smaller needle.

construction
The hood is worked flat, binding off stitches on the sides while keeping the middle stitches live to create a gusset (which is sewn together at the end). Stitches are picked up in the round at the base of the hood and worked in rib. The drawstring and tassel are made separately. Sew a coordinating hood lining (see page 75) and handsew it into the hood.

notes
Keep first and last stitch of hood in reverse stockinette stitch throughout for selvedge.
Bind off all stitches in pattern.

stitch guide

Make bobble (MB): (Knit into front, back, front, back) of same st (4 new sts on right needle), pass first 3 sts over last st on right needle—1 st rem.

3/3 RC: Sl 3 sts onto cn and hold in back, k3, k3 from cn.

3/3 LC: Sl 3 sts onto cn and hold in front, k3, k3 from cn.

Cable Pattern: (mult 12 sts + 11)
Row 1: (RS) P1, *3/3 RC, k3, p1, MB, p1; rep from * to last 10 sts, 3/3 RC, k3, p1.
Rows 2–4: Work sts as they appear.
Row 5: P1, *k3, 3/3 LC, p1, k1, p1; rep from * to last 10 sts, k3, 3/3 LC, p1.
Rows 6–8: Work sts as they appear.
Rep Rows 1–8 for patt.

Cable Bind-Off 3 Front (CBO3F): Sl 3 sts onto cn and hold in front of next 3 sts on left needle, [knit first st on cn tog with first st on left needle, pass next st on right needle over this st to BO] 3 times—6 sts total BO.

Cable Bind-Off 3 Back (CBO3B): Sl 3 sts onto cn and hold in back of next 3 sts on left needle, [knit first st on left needle tog with first st on cn, pass next st on right needle over this st to BO] 3 times—6 sts total BO.

HOOD

With smaller needle, CO 215 sts. Work Rows 1–8 of cable patt (see Stitch Guide), then work Row 1 once more.

Next row: (turning row) Knit. Piece measures about 1½" (3.8 cm).

Change to larger needle. Work Rows 3–8 of cable patt, then work Rows 1–6 of cable patt once more.

hem

Fold CO edge along turning row with WS tog. Join CO edge to working sts in patt as foll: For each knit st, insert right needle through next st on left needle, then through next CO st; pull new st through. For each purl st, insert right needle through next CO st, then through next st on left needle; pull new st through. Work in this manner across row—215 sts.

Work Row 8 of cable patt, then work Rows 1–8 again.

shaping

Work Row 1 of cable patt.

Cont in patt, BO 4 sts at beg of next 6 rows—191 sts rem.
Work 6 rows even in patt as established.

Cont in patt, BO 4 sts at beg of next 6 rows—167 sts rem.
Work even in patt for 25 rows.

back of hood

Next row: BO 3 sts, CBO3F, BO 6 sts, CBO3F, BO 3 sts (24 sts BO; last st worked is a purl st), work next 36 sts in patt as established (37 sts on right needle), BO 2 sts, CBO3F, cut yarn and pull through last st on right needle—37 sts rem on right needle; sl rem 97 sts from left needle to holder.

right edge
Next row: With WS facing, join yarn and work 37 sts in patt.
Work in patt for 2 more rows.

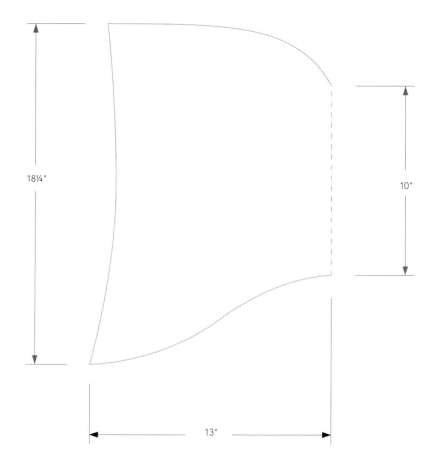

18¼"

13"

10"

Enlarge 500%

Next row: P1, CBO3B, BO 6 sts, work
  in patt to end of row—25 sts rem.
Work 3 rows even in patt.

Next row: (RS) BO 3 sts, CBO3F, BO 6
  sts, CBO3F, BO last 4 sts—no sts rem.

left edge
Keep 27 sts at center of piece on holder;
place last 70 sts on larger needle.

Next row: BO 2 sts, CBO3F, BO 1 st,
  work next 36 sts in patt (37 sts on right
  needle), BO 4 sts, CBO3F, BO 6 sts,
  CBO3F, BO last st, cut yarn and pull
  through last st on right needle—37 sts
  rem.

Next row: With WS facing, join yarn and
  work to end of row in patt.
Work 2 rows even in patt.

Next row: (RS) Work in patt for 25 sts,
  BO 1 st, CBO3B, BO last 4 sts, cut
  yarn and pull through final st on right
  needle—25 sts rem.
Work 3 rows even in patt.

Next row: BO 5 sts, CBO3F, BO 6 sts, CBO3F, BO last st—no sts rem.

gusset

Place 27 held sts on larger needle. Mark this row using a locking-ring marker. With RS facing, join yarn.

Beg with Row 5, work even in cable patt until piece measures 15" (38 cm) from marked row, ending with Row 4 of patt.

Row 5: BO 5 sts, CBO3F, BO 6 sts, CBO3F, BO last 3 sts—no sts rem.

attach gusset to sides

Beg at bottom of gusset and using bobbles as a guide, pin right edge and left edge of back of hood to gusset selvedge edges, keeping cables from right edge and left edge aligned. With yarn threaded on a tapestry needle, use mattress stitch (see Glossary, page 131) to sew pieces together.

rib yoke

Mark center of BO edge of gusset with locking-ring marker. With smaller cir, RS facing, hood upside down, and beg at inside of base of hem, pick up and knit 75 sts evenly spaced to m, then pick up and knit 75 sts from m to opposite edge—150 sts total. Place marker (pm) and join for working in the rnd.

Rnd 1: *K2, p1; rep from * to end.
Rep Rnd 1 until piece measures 6" (15 cm) from picked up edge. With larger cir, BO all sts.

lining

Fold lining fabric in half. Enlarge pattern (see page 73) 500% and use it to cut out fabric for lining, placing fold at back of head. (See Sewing for Knitters, opposite.) Using a ½" (1.3 cm) seam allowance, sew top of hood lining by hand or sewing machine. Turn under and sew a ½" (1.3 cm) hem along hood opening and picked-up sts for rib yoke. Finish cut edges. Pin lining into hood aligning with top of rib and along seam from knitted hem. Backstitch (see Glossary, page 130) lining to hood opening and base of cable portion, following stitching line of hem.

drawstring

With smaller dpn and leaving a 9" (23 cm) tail, CO 3 sts. Work I-cord (see Glossary, page 129) for 44" (112 cm). BO all sts and cut yarn, leaving a 9" (23 cm) tail. Pass I-cord through tube formed by hem. Thread tail on tapestry needle and string wooden bead. Rep for second tail and bead.

tassel *(make 2)*

Wrap yarn around cardboard 24 times; cut yarn. Thread tail from drawstring through top of tassel between cardboard and yarn to secure loops (see Glossary, page 132). Wrap tail through and around loops at top of tassel twice, then around strand between tassel and bead twice. Remove tassel from cardboard. Wrap yarn 6 times around tassel ¼–½" (6–13 mm) below top to form tassel throat. Sew through tassel throat securely. Cut loops at bottom of tassel and trim even.

SEWING FOR KNITTERS

You can already do great things with yarn and knitting needles. But to take your knitted pieces to the next level, it's helpful to learn a few techniques that involve thread and a sewing needle.

Some stitches, like backstitch, whipstitch, and running stitch, are common to sewing and knitting. These very useful stitches are common in knitting and usually given in a standard knitting glossary (see pages 127–132).

Three of the projects in this book—the Hoodie Devoted (page 70), Pleated Denim Purse (page 110), and Big Brown Bag (page 80)—are lined with fabric. Each project gives specific sewing directions, but there are some basics that will help make sewing a more enjoyable experience.

TOOLS AND MATERIALS

Handsewing needles

Tweezers

Seam ripper

Ball-head pins

Pin cushion

Sharp scissors and/or rotary cutter and mat

Flat surface

Sewing machine (optional)

Pinking shears (optional)

GENERAL SEWING TIPS

+ If the finished piece might be washed, wash and dry the fabric before cutting and sewing. This will prevent it from running or shrinking and ruining your finished piece in the wash.

+ Always press your fabric before cutting and sewing, using an iron on the appropriate setting for the fabric you're using.

+ Always mark or draw on the wrong side of the fabric.

+ When sewing on a machine, be careful that the needle doesn't run over any pins, or you may break the needle and damage the machine.

+ Basting is a method of holding fabric in place with loose stitches. It's intended to be removed when the pieces are secure and the final seams are made. It's a good idea to use a contrasting thread and long running stitch to baste pieces together before sewing to hold them steady and make sure the finished piece will work as you intended.

+ A magnet can be handy to gather up spilled pins—these have a nasty habit of winding up where you least expect them.

+ Most sewing patterns include a seam allowance— the distance between the edge of the fabric and where the seam is intended to go—of ½–⅝" (1.3–1.5 cm). When sewing your own pattern, leave at least ½" (1.3 cm) seam allowance.

+ Cut edges of fabric tend to ravel, and when pressure is put on the fabric at a seam, it can pull apart. To avoid splitting seams, finish the edges of fabric by using pinking shears to cut zigzags or sewing along the edge with the zigzag stitch on your sewing machine.

+ Sewing a woven lining into a knitted piece will provide some stability, so keep in mind that the woven fabric will not allow the knit fabric to stretch freely. When machine-sewing a knitted fabric to a woven fabric, be sure that the knitted fabric is moving at the same speed as the woven fabric, or you will end up with a bunchy seam. It is a good idea to pin or baste the fabrics before stitching and gently guide both fabrics through the machine, checking for any bunching as you stitch.

HEATHER HEADBAND

I wanted to create a knitted piece around a preexisting shape that would hold up for a long time without stretching. This sweet headband of asymmetrical cables and bobbles that meet and redirect on the sides suits the needs of a smart dresser. An instant classic.

finished size
16½" (42 cm) long and 3" (7.5 cm) wide at widest point.

yarn
Laceweight (Lace #0).
Shown here: GGH Tajmahal (70% wool, 22% silk, 8% cashmere; 93 yd [85 m]/25 g): #12 charcoal, 1 skein.

needles
U.S. size 1 (2.25 mm). Adjust needle size if necessary to obtain the correct gauge.

notions
Cable needle (cn); 1½ × 15" (3.8 × 38 cm) plastic headband; tapestry needle.

gauge
11 sts and 11 rows = 1" (2.5 cm) in cable patt.

construction
The piece is worked flat in one piece, using much smaller needles than usual for this yarn to create a tighter fabric. The finished knitted piece is seamed around a plastic headband.

stitch guide

Bobble: (K1, p1, k1, p1) into the same st (4 new sts on right needle), pass first 3 sts over last st on right needle—1 st rem.

HEATHER HEADBAND

HEADBAND

CO 14 sts.

Work Rows 1–138 of Headband chart.

Next row: (bind-off row) K1, ssk, pass knit st over ssk to BO 1 st, BO all sts to last 3 sts, k2tog, pass st over k2tog to BO 1 st, k1, pass k2tog over knit st to BO 1 st. Fasten off last st—no sts rem.

FINISHING

With yarn threaded on a tapestry needle, use mattress st (see Glossary, page 131) to join edges of piece for three-fourths of its length. Slip headband inside sewn portion and sew to end.

Headband Chart

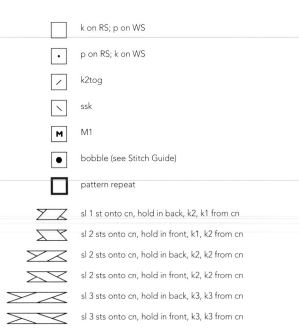

- ☐ k on RS; p on WS
- • p on RS; k on WS
- ╱ k2tog
- ╲ ssk
- **M** M1
- ● bobble (see Stitch Guide)
- ☐ pattern repeat
- sl 1 st onto cn, hold in back, k2, k1 from cn
- sl 2 sts onto cn, hold in front, k1, k2 from cn
- sl 2 sts onto cn, hold in back, k2, k2 from cn
- sl 2 sts onto cn, hold in front, k2, k2 from cn
- sl 3 sts onto cn, hold in back, k3, k3 from cn
- sl 3 sts onto cn, hold in front, k3, k3 from cn

work 2x

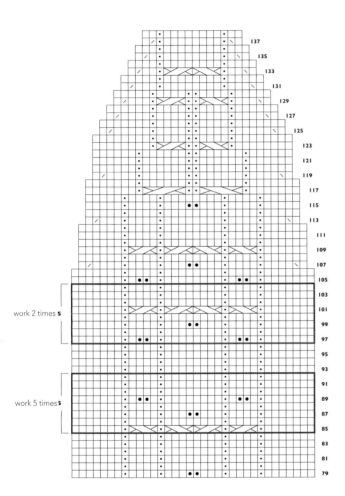

work 2 times **s**

work 5 times **s**

137
135
133
131
129
127
125
123
121
119
117
115
113
111
109
107
105
103
101
99
97
95
93
91
89
87
85
83
81
79

BIG BROWN BAG

The secret of felting is that in order to get the shape you want, you have to create it after you've finished knitting and felting. I used a number of props to keep this bag in shape. Inspired by leather handbags, I found plenty of hardware and adornment to polish off the charming look.

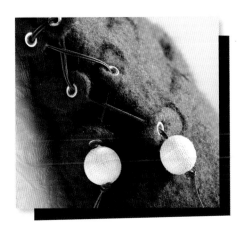

finished size
36" (91.5 cm) circumference at top of bag, 48" (122 cm) circumference at base of bag, and 26" (66 cm) tall before felting; 24" (61 cm) circumference at top of bag, 32" (81.5 cm) circumference at base of bag, and 12" (30.5 cm) tall after felting.

yarn
Worsted weight (Medium #4).
Shown here: Berroco Ultra Alpaca (50% alpaca, 50% wool; 215 yd [197 m]/100 g): #6205 dark chocolate, 4 skeins.

needles
U.S. size 10½ (6.5 mm): 24" (60 cm) circular (cir) and set of 2 double-pointed (dpn). Adjust needle size if necessary to obtain the correct gauge.

notions
4 × 14" (10 × 35.5 cm) cardboard; plastic bag; ¼ yd (.25 m) Timtex interfacing material; ¼ yd (.25 m) lining fabric; sewing thread to match fabric; 6 small stitch holders; 3 same-colored markers (m), plus 1 one of a different color; cotton waste yarn (for felting); mesh laundry bags or pillowcases with zipper; four ¼" (6 mm) nickel Chicago screws; 92" (2.3 m) of 1.25 mm leather lacing, cut into four equal lengths; four 1" (2.5 cm) cream woven fabric round beads; four 1¼" (3.2 cm) horseshoe nickel handle hooks; Set-it Yourself Grommet Kit No. K231 Size 00; mallet or small hammer; flat-head screwdriver; razor blade (optional); sewing machine (for lining).

gauge
16 sts and 18½ rnds = 4" (10 cm) in St st before felting; 24 sts and 40 rnds = 4" (10 cm) in St st after felting.

construction
Begin the bag by knitting the base, then pick up stitches for the sides and work upward. Knit pleats, three loop rows, and horseshoe hook straps. Knit two shoulder straps and six horizontal straps separately. Felt, shape, and assemble.

stitch guide

Make pleat: Slip next 6 sts from left needle onto dpn and hold in front of next 6 sts on left needle, [knit first st from dpn tog with first st from left needle] 6 times, slip next 6 sts from left needle to dpn and hold in back of next 6 sts on left needle, [knit first st from left needle tog with first st from dpn] 6 times.

BAG

bottom
With cir needle, CO 72 sts.

Beg with a RS row, work in St st for 33 rows, ending with a RS row. Do not turn work.

sides
Rotate piece, place marker (pm), pick up and knit 24 sts along selvedge edge, pm, pick up and knit 72 sts along CO edge, pm, pick up and knit 24 sts along selvedge edge—192 sts total. Place different-colored marker to indicate beg of rnd and join for working in the rnd. Knit 48 rnds.

box pleats
Next rnd: *K8, make pleat (see Stitch Guide), k8, make pleat, k8, sl m, k24, sl m; rep from * once more—144 sts rem.
Knit 1 rnd.

loop setup
Loop setup rnd: *K8 and place last 8 sts worked on a holder, k20 and place last 8 sts worked on another holder, k20 and place last 8 sts worked on another holder, sl m, k24, sl m; rep from * once more—96 sts rem.
Next rnd: Using the knitted method (see Glossary, page 127), *CO 8 sts, k12, CO 8 sts, k12, CO 8 sts, sl m, k24, sl m; rep from * once more—144 sts.
Knit 10 rnds.

make loops
Place first set of 8 held sts on dpn. *With a separate strand of yarn and leaving a 12" (30.5 cm) tail, work these 8 sts in St st for 10 rows, ending with a WS row. Cut yarn. Hold 8 sts on dpn in front of first 8 sts on left cir needle. With original working yarn, [knit first st on dpn tog with first st on cir] 8 times*, k12, place next set of 8 held sts on dpn, rep from * to *, k12, place next set of 8 held sts on dpn, rep from * to *, sl m, k24, sl m, place next set of 8 held sts on dpn, rep from * to *, k12, place next set of 8 held sts on dpn, rep from * to *, k12, place last set of 8 held sts on dpn, rep from * to *, sl m, k24. Work 10 rnds even.

Rep loop setup and make loops sections 2 more times—3 rows of 6 loops.

bind off and horseshoe hook straps
K8 and place these 8 sts on a holder, BO all sts to 7 sts before m, k7 and place 8 sts from right needle onto second holder, remove m, BO all sts to next m, remove m, knit until there are 8 sts on right needle and place these 8 sts on third holder, BO all sts to 7 sts before m, k7 and place 8 sts from right needle onto fourth holder, remove m, BO all sts to end of rnd, remove m—32 sts rem on 4 holders.

horseshoe hook straps
Place sts from one holder on needles and, beg with a RS row, work 10 rows in St st, then BO all sts. Rep for rem 3 holders.

HORIZONTAL STRAPS *(make 6)*
CO 6 sts.

Row 1: (inc row; RS) K1, k1f&b, knit to last 2 sts, k1f&b, k1—8 sts.
Row 2: Purl.
Rep Rows 1 and 2 once more—10 sts.
Work in St st for 76 rows, ending with a WS row.

Next row: (dec row) K1, ssk, k4, k2tog, k1—8 sts rem.
Next row: Purl.
Next row: (bind-off row) K1, ssk, pass knit st over ssk to BO 1 st, BO all sts to last 3 sts, k2tog, pass st over k2tog to BO 1 st, k1, pass k2tog over knit st to BO 1 st. Fasten off last st—no sts rem.

shoulder straps *(make 2)*
CO 6 sts.
Beg with a RS row, work 10 rows in St st, ending with a WS row.

Next row: (inc row) K1, k1f&b, knit to last 2 sts, k1f&b, k1—8 sts.
Next row: Purl.
Next row: Rep inc row—10 sts.
Work in St st until piece measures 32" (81.5 cm) from CO, ending with a WS row.

Next row: (dec row) K1, ssk, knit to last 3 sts, k2tog, k1—8 sts rem.
Next row: Purl.
Next row: Rep dec row—6 sts rem.
Work in St st for 9 rows. BO all sts.

FINISHING

horseshoe hook straps

Fold horseshoe hook straps in half with WS tog. With yarn threaded on a tapestry needle, whipstitch (see Glossary, page 131) BO end of strap to top of bag. Turn bag inside out. With tail threaded on a tapestry needle, use whipstitch to sew the opening at the bottom of each loop closed. Weave in loose ends.

felt

With cotton yarn, tie a loop loosely but firmly through each loop and horseshoe hook strap to prevent openings from felting shut.

Place bag and shoulder straps in separate pillowcases or lingerie bags. Wash on shortest, hottest cycle and lowest water level. (See page 21 for information on felting.) Check piece for degree of felting every 5 minutes; if necessary, reset the washing machine to begin again, but do not allow the piece to go through a rinse or spin cycle. When it is sufficiently felted, remove the piece from the washer and shape to measurements. Allow to dry completely.

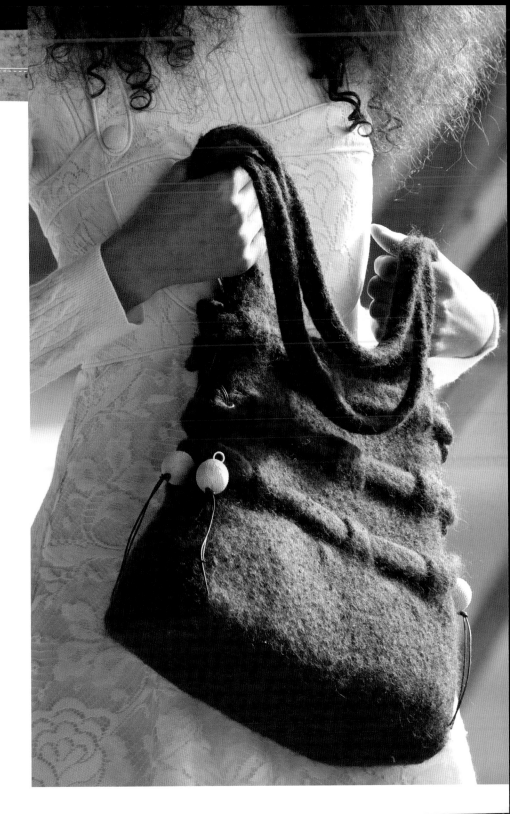

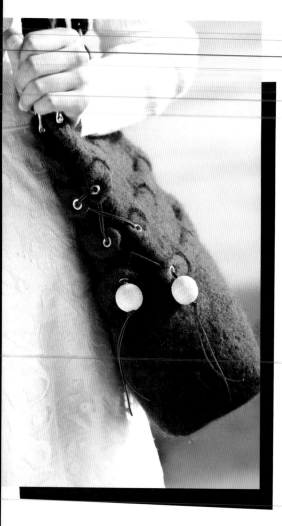

after felting

shape and dry

Remove bag and straps from washer
and roll up in a towel to remove excess
water. Shape and stretch bag and straps
to desired measurements. Remove
cotton waste yarn and use your hands or
a dpn to be sure the loops and horseshoe
straps have not felted shut. If necessary,
you can use a razor blade to cut a felted
area open, but be cautious.

While pieces are still damp, place
cardboard inside plastic bag, insert in
bottom of felted bag, and shape felted
bag to measurements.

If necessary, you can iron, rewet, and/or
steam the felt for additional shaping.

attach hooks to loops

Remove the screw from each horseshoe
hook, pass 1 screw through 1 loop at top
of bag, and re-close horseshoe hook
(see opposite). Repeat for 3 remaining
hooks and loops. With RS of bag facing,
insert 1¼" (3.2 cm) of shoulder strap
through horseshoe hook and fold toward
WS of strap. Pass the Chicago screw
post through both layers of the strap
(use hole cutter from grommet set if
necessary) and secure, using a
screwdriver to tighten (see opposite).

attach horizontal straps

Working on a solid and stable surface,
use hole cutter from grommet kit to
make a small hole ½" (1.3 cm) from
each end of each horizontal strap—
12 holes total (see opposite). Follow
instructions on grommet kit to insert
grommets in each hole and secure. Pass
each horizontal strap through 1 set of
side loops so that grommets sit at sides
of bag. With 2 pieces of leather lacing
held together and beg with top straps,
alternate passing through the grommets
on one end of bag as if lacing up shoes.
Repeat lacing on other end of bag.
Insert ends of leather lacing through
beads and secure with overhand knots.
Trim ends of lacing as desired.

bottom insert

Cut two 4 × 14" (10 × 35.5 cm) pieces
of interfacing. Cut lining fabric to 15 ×
9" (38 × 23 cm). Fold fabric lengthwise
with right sides together. Using a ½"
(1.3 cm) seam allowance, sew long edge
and one short edge. Turn fabric right-
side out. Insert interfacing into fabric,
fitting into corners. Fold excess fabric
from unfinished short side to inside of
fabric bag. Topstitch short side closed.
Place in bottom of bag for stability.

HORSESHOE HOOKS & GROMMETS

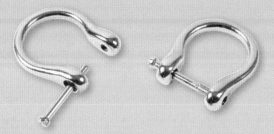

HORSESHOE HANDLE HOOKS

Sometimes I look for hardware because I have a need to fulfill. For the Big Brown Bag, I needed some hardware that would attach the handles to the bag. When I found the horseshoe nickel handle hook, it was perfection. I hadn't known what I was looking for, but I knew it when I found it!

These amazing little devices are borrowed from leatherwork, where they hold straps with side-to-side holes on purses. They're perfect to attach bags and handles after felting, and they don't even require much planning. They look like horseshoes with a horizontal post that closes the top of the horseshoe. The end of the post is threaded. To use it, remove the horizontal screw with a small screwdriver or your fingers. Slide the horseshoe part through one of the pieces to be joined. Slide the screw through the larger hole on the side of the hook, then pass it through the other piece to be joined and screw it into the other side of the horseshoe. Use the screwdriver to secure the screw. (If the pieces are flexible, it may be easier to push both of them onto the horseshoe portion, screw in the post, and slide the bottom piece over the post.)

GROMMETS

Grommets reinforce the holes in fabric, giving felt a clean and finished look. They are made up of two pieces, the grommet and the washer. Complete grommet kits are available at craft and fabric stores; they may include a wooden block, special pliers, or a hole cutter to make the process easier.

To insert grommets, make sure you are working on a stable and solid surface. Using the hole cutter from the kit, a razor blade, or the grommet itself, make a hole in the desired location and place the grommet in the hole on the right side. Turn the piece over so that the wrong side is facing and the grommet is lying on top of the inserting base. (Some kits include a set of pliers instead of an inserting base and die; in that case, place the holes of the washer and grommet directly between the jaws of the pliers.) Place the washer on top of the grommet and place the holes of the washer and grommet between the inserting die and the inside of the inserting base. Put all of the pieces on top of the wood block, then use a mallet or hammer to tap the washer and grommet into place.

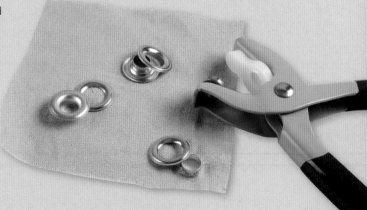

BRAIDED CABLE BELT

Make friends with appliqué. The pull-through straps on this sleek belt are double-sided, keeping them tidy and curl-free. This belt is meant to sit high on the waist over a top or thin sweater, not be pulled through belt loops.

finished size
3" (7.5 cm) wide and customizable length. Cable section of belt shown measures 23" (58.5 cm).

yarn
Worsted weight (Medium #4).
Shown here: GGH Scarlett (100% cotton; 120 yd [110 m]/50 g): #22 gray, 2 balls.

needles
U.S. size 3 (3.25 mm). Adjust needle size if necessary to obtain the correct gauge.

notions
U.S. size E/4 (3.5 mm) crochet hook; small cable needle (cn); small stitch holder; 4 sewing pins or T-pins; tapestry needle; two 1 × 1½" (2.5 × 3.8 cm) nickel buckles.

gauge
32 sts and 16 rows = 3" (7.5 cm) in cable patt.

construction
The belt is begun with two buckle straps, which grow into the cabled section. The pull-through appliqué section and crocheted belt loops are made separately.

stitch guide

2/2 LC: Sl 2 sts onto cn and hold in front, k2, k2 from cn.

2/2 RC: Sl 2 sts onto cn and hold in back, k2, k2 from cn.

BELT

buckle straps

CO 6 sts.

Row 1: K1, k1f&b, knit to last 2 sts, k1f&b, k1—8 sts.

Row 2 and all WS rows: Purl.

Row 3: Rep Row 1—10 sts.

Rows 4–18: Work in St st, ending with a WS row.

Place sts on holder; cut yarn. Rep entire section for second buckle strap but do not place sts on holder.

attach straps

With RS of second strap facing and using the knitted method (see Glossary, page 127), CO 4 sts, then purl across all sts—14 sts total.

Turn work and, using the knitted method, CO 4 sts—18 sts total.

Turn work so RS is facing and purl held sts of strap—28 sts total.

Turn work so WS is facing and, using the knitted method, CO 4 sts—32 sts total.

CABLE SECTION

Note: WS of buckle strap is RS of cable section.

Row 1: (RS) *2/2 LC (see Stitch Guide); rep from * to end.

Rows 2–4: Work in St st.

Row 5: K2, *2/2 RC (see Stitch Guide); rep from * to last 2 sts, k2.

Rows 6–8: Work in St st.

Rep Rows 1-8 until cable section measures 4" (10 cm) less than actual waist measurement, ending with Row 1. With WS facing, BO all sts.

PULL-THROUGH STRAP APPLIQUÉ

CO 14 sts.

Row 1: (RS) K1, k1f&b, knit to last 2 sts, k1f&b, k1—16 sts.

Row 2: Purl.

Rows 3–6: Rep Rows 1 and 2 two more times—20 sts at the end of Row 6.

Work 10 rows even in St st.

Next row: (RS) K8 and place these 8 sts on a holder for second strap, BO 4 sts, knit to end of row—8 sts rem.

pull-through strap

Work in St st for 19 rows, ending with a WS row.

Next row: (RS) K1, ssk, knit to last 3 sts, k2tog, k1—6 sts rem.

Next row: Purl.

Next row: K1, ssk, k2tog, k1—4 sts rem.

Next row: Purl.

Next row: K1, k1f&b, k1f&b, k1—6 sts.

Next row: Purl.

Next row: K1, k1f&b, knit to last 2 sts, k1f&b, k1—8 sts.

Work in St st for 23 rows. BO.

With WS facing, place 8 held sts onto needles. Reattach yarn and rep pull-through strap section.

BELT LOOP (make 2)

With crochet hook, make slip knot, chain 10 (see Glossary, page 128), and fasten off. Cut yarn, leaving an 8" (20.5 cm) tail.

WS of belt with appliqué

RS of belt with appliqué

FINISHING
Block as desired.

buckle straps
With RS of belt facing, pass buckle strap through bottom of buckle from WS to RS. Fold straps over belt, trapping buckles at start of cable section. If necessary, use pins to keep the straps even. With yarn threaded on a tapestry needle, use running st (see Glossary, page 131) to sew straps to belt along the strap edges, sewing between the first and second stitches of the strap. Weave in loose ends.

attach crochet belt loops
Measure ¾" (2 cm) from fold of buckle strap for belt loop placement. With tail threaded on a tapestry needle, sew belt loop across buckle strap. Pull ends to WS of belt and fasten very securely, knotting if necessary.

pull-through strap appliqué
With RS of belt facing, lay large end of appliqué on top of belt end, centering appliqué on ends of cable section and lining up 4 BO center sts with end of cable section. Pin pieces in place. With yarn threaded on a tapestry needle, use a running stitch to sew base of appliqué to belt around edges. Fold WS of each pull-through strap onto itself at narrowest point and sew sides of each strap tog. Use whipstitch (see Glossary, page 131) to sew BO end of each strap to WS of belt.

PLAIN TALK
RUFFLED
MITTENS

The cuffs of these mittens are long enough to stay tucked under a coat sleeve (with a little ruffle peeking out) or over the sleeves of a top or sweater. Despite the buttons and ruffles, these mittens remain understated and clean. Suede palms and thumbs give you a steady grip.

finished size
11¾" (30 cm) long and 7½" (19 cm) hand circumference.

yarn
Worsted weight (Medium #4). *Shown here:* Mission Falls 1824 Wool (100% superwash merino wool; 85 yd [78 m]/50 g): #006 oatmeal (dark tan), 3 balls, and #002 stone (light tan), 1 ball.

needles
U.S. size 4 (3.5 mm): straight and set of 5 double-pointed (dpn). U.S. size 5 (3.75 mm): straight. U.S. size 6 (4 mm): straight and dpn. Adjust needle size if necessary to obtain the correct gauge.

notions
Two markers; stitch holder; ten ½" (1.3 cm) buttons; sewing needle and matching thread; suede mitten palms and thumb tips; tapestry needle.

gauge
21 sts and 30 rnds = 4" (10 cm) in St st on largest needles.

construction
The mittens are worked flat for the cuff, then in the round to the tips of the fingers, with stitches held to work the thumb later. Add the ruffle by picking up stitches along the cuff.

RIGHT MITTEN

cuff

With dark tan and largest straight needles, CO 45 sts.

Row 1: (RS) K6, *p1, k3; rep from * to last 3 sts, p1, k2.

Row 2: Work in rib patt as established.

Row 3: (buttonhole row) K3, yo, k2tog, k1, work in patt to end of row.

Rows 4–10: Work even in rib pattern.

Row 11: Change to middle-size needles and rep Row 3 (buttonhole row).

Rep Rows 4–11 once.

Rep Rows 4–7 once more.

Change to smallest needles and rep Rows 8–10, then rep Rows 3–11 once more—5 buttonholes. Work 1 WS row in rib patt as established.

join cuff

Change to smallest dpns and work next row in patt, distributing sts as foll: *Needle 1:* Work 13 sts; *Needle 2:* Work 6 sts, place marker (pm), work 1 st, pm, work 6 sts; *Needle 3:* Work 13 sts; *Needle 4:* Sl 6 sts onto needle without working.

Hold Needle 4 with 6 unworked stitches behind Needle 1. With an empty needle, [knit first st on Needle 1 tog with first st on Needle 4] 6 times, then work rem 7 sts of Needle 1 in patt—39 sts rem. Work to end of Needle 3 in patt.

Change to largest needles and St st. Work to first m (beg of rnd).

gusset

Setup rnd: Sl m, M1 (see Glossary, page 129), k1, M1, sl m, knit to end of rnd—41 sts total; 3 sts between m.

Rnds 1 and 2: Work even.

Rnd 3: Sl m, M1, knit to m, M1, sl m, knit to end of rnd—2 sts inc'd.

Rep Rnds 1–3 three more times—49 sts total; 11 sts between m.

Work 3 rnds even.

Rep Rnd 3—51 sts total; 13 sts between m.

Next rnd: Remove m, sl 13 sts to holder for thumb, remove m, use the backward loop method (see Glossary, page 127) to CO 1 st, pm for beg of rnd, knit to end of rnd—39 sts rem. Work even in St st until piece measures 5" (12.5 cm) from beg of St st.

shape tip

Rnd 1: Ssk, k16, k2tog, pm, ssk, knit to last 2 sts, k2tog—35 sts rem.

Rnd 2: Knit.

Rnd 3: Ssk, knit to 2 sts before m, k2tog, ssk, knit to last 2 sts, k2tog—4 sts dec'd.

Rnd 4: Knit.

Rep Rnds 3 and 4 three more times—19 sts rem.

Rep Rnd 3 three times—7 sts rem.

Pull tail through rem sts and fasten off inside.

thumb

Place 13 held thumb sts onto largest dpns, pick up and knit 1 st in CO st, pm and join for working in the rnd—14 sts. Work in St st for 12 rnds.

shape thumb tip

Rnd 1: K2tog, k4, k2tog, k4, k2tog—11 sts rem.

Rnd 2: Knit.

Rnd 3: K2tog, k3, k2tog, k2, k2tog—8 sts rem.

Rnd 4: Knit.

Rnd 5: K2tog, k1, k2tog, k1, k2tog—5 sts rem.

Pull tail through rem sts and fasten off inside.

ruffle

With middle-size needles, dark tan, RS facing, and beg at CO edge, pick up and knit 26 sts along buttonhole edge of cuff.

Row 1: Purl.

Row 2: P2, M1, k3, [p2, M1, k2] 4 times, p2, M1, k3—32 sts.

Row 3 and all odd-numbered rows: Work in rib patt as established, purling new sts.

Row 4: P2, M1, k4, [p2, M1, k3] 4 times, p2, M1, k4—38 sts.

Row 6: Change to light tan. P2, M1, k5, [p2, M1, k4] 4 times, p2, M1, k5—44 sts.

Row 8: P2, M1, k6, [p2, M1, k5] 4

times, p2, M1, k6—50 sts.
With WS facing, BO all sts in patt.

LEFT MITTEN

cuff

With dark tan and largest straight
needles, CO 45 sts.

Row 1: (RS) K2, p1, k3, *p1, k3; rep
from * to last 3 sts, k3.

Row 2: Work in rib patt as established.

Row 3: (buttonhole row) Work in patt
to last 6 sts, k2, yo, k2tog, k2.

Beg with row 4, work as for right
mitten cuff, ending with a WS row.

join cuff

Change to smallest dpns and work next
row in patt, distributing sts as foll:
Needle 1: Work 13 sts; *Needle 2:* Work 11
sts; *Needle 3:* Work 1 st, pm, work 1 st,
pm, work 13 sts; *Needle 4:* Sl 6 sts onto
needle without working. Hold Needle
4 in front of Needle 1 and, with an
empty needle, [knit first st on Needle
4 tog with first st on Needle 1] 6
times—39 sts rem. Work in patt to end
of Needle 3.
Change to largest dpns and St st. Work
to first m (beg of rnd).

Beg with gusset, work as for right
mitten for remainder of hand and
thumb.

ruffle

With middle-size needles, dark tan,
RS facing, and beg at cuff join, pick up
and knit 26 sts along buttonhole edge
of cuff.

Row 1: Purl.

Row 2: K3, M1, p2, [k2, M1, p2] 4
times, k3, M1, p2—32 sts.

Row 3 and all odd-numbered rows:
Work in rib patt as established,
purling new sts.

Row 4: K4, M1, p2, [k3, M1, p2] 4
times, k4, M1, p2—38 sts.

Row 6: Change to light tan. K5, M1,
p2, [k4, M1, p2] 4 times, k5, M1,
p2—44 sts.

Row 8: K6, M1, p2, [k5, M1, p2] 4
times, k6, M1, p2—50 sts.

With WS facing, BO all sts in patt.

FINISHING

Weave in loose ends. With sewing
needle and thread, sew buttons
opposite buttonholes. Use backstitch
(see Glossary, page 130) to sew suede
mitten palms to palms of mittens near
mitten tips and suede thumb tips to
ends of thumbs.

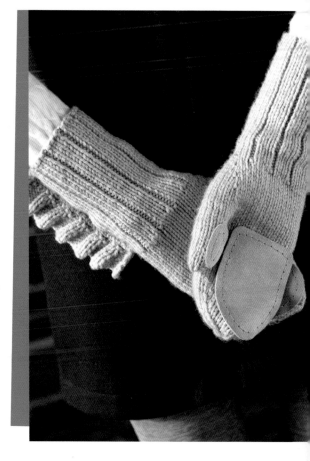

WHISKEY FELTED CAP

A millinery apprenticeship helped me take my felted hats to the next level. Discovering shaping on hat blocks opened up a world of possibilities, but most people don't have hat blocks, so I decided to build one without the block. As with all felting, the shaping afterwards is necessary to the success of the piece.

finished size
24¾" (63 cm) circumference before felting; 21½" (54.5 cm) circumference after felting. To fit 21½–22" (54.5–56 cm) head circumference.

yarn
Sportweight (Fine #2). *Shown here:* Reynolds Whiskey (100% wool; 195 yd [178 m]/50 g): #103 light olive, 2 balls.

needles
U.S. size 9 (5.5 mm): 16" (40 cm) circular (cir) and set of 4 or 5 double-pointed (dpn). U.S. size 5 (3.75 mm): straight. Adjust needle size if necessary to obtain the correct gauge.

notions
Markers (m); stitch holder; two ¾" (2 cm) D-rings; sewing pins; 24" (61 cm) of 2¾" (7 cm) wide satin ribbon; 24" (61 cm) of ⅞" (2.2 cm) wide grosgrain ribbon; sewing needle and thread to match grosgrain ribbon and yarn; custom label (optional; see page 99); iron and ironing board; washing machine; lingerie bag or pillowcase with zipper.

gauge
20 sts and 26 rnds = 4" (10 cm) in St st on larger needle before felting.
23 sts and 42 rnds = 4" (10 cm) in St st on larger needle after felting.
24 sts and 32 rows = 4" (10 cm) in St st on smaller needles.

construction
The hat is worked back and forth in rows for the bill, then in the round to the crown with short-row shaping for the peak. The body of the hat is felted, and an unfelted band is attached to hold a bow. The inside is finished with a grosgrain ribbon and optional custom label (see page 99).

HAT

bill

With larger needle, CO 34 sts. Do not join.

Row 1: (RS) K1f&b, knit to last st, k1f&b—2 sts inc'd.

Row 2: Purl.

Rep Rows 1 and 2 four more times—44 sts.

Next row: Knit.

body

Using the knitted method (see Glossary, page 127), CO 80 sts, place marker (pm), and, with RS facing, join for working in the rnd, being careful not to twist sts—124 sts.

Knit 4 rnds.

Next rnd: K79, sl next 10 sts to holder; using the knitted method, CO 10 sts; with RS facing, knit to end of rnd.

Knit 20 rnds.

loop

Next rnd: K79. Cut yarn.

Place held sts onto 1 dpn. Join yarn and work in St st for 20 rows, ending with a WS row.

Hold dpn in front of next 10 sts on left cir needle and, using cir needle, [knit 1 st from dpn tog with 1 st from left needle] 10 times, knit to end of rnd.

Knit 20 rnds.

shape peak

Shape the front of the hat using short-rows (see Glossary, page 132) as foll, working wraps tog with wrapped sts when you come to them.

Short-row 1: (RS) K34, wrap next st, turn.

Short-row 2: (WS) P24, wrap next st, turn.

Short-row 3: K25, wrap next st, turn.

Short-row 4: P26, wrap next st, turn.

Continue in this manner, working 1 additional st on every short row, for 16 more rows, ending with a WS row—42 sts between wraps.

Knit 2 rnds, working wraps tog with wrapped sts as you come to them.

crown

Rnd 1: *K29, k2tog; rep from * 3 more times—120 sts rem.

Rnds 2 and 3: Knit.

Rnd 4: *K28, k2tog; rep from * 3 more times—116 sts rem.

Rnds 5 and 6: Knit.

Rnd 7: (turning rnd) Purl.

Rnd 8: (turning ridge) *Insert needle into first stitch as if to knit, then under the purl bump below the turning rnd (on inside of hat), and knit these 2 sts tog; rep from * to end of rnd.

Rnd 9: *K27, k2tog; rep from * 3 more times—112 sts rem.

Rnd 10: *K12, k2tog, pm; rep from * 7 more times—104 sts rem.

Rnd 11: Knit.

Rnd 12: *Knit to 2 sts before m, k2tog; rep from * 7 more times—8 sts dec'd.

Rep Rnds 11 and 12 ten more times, changing to dpn when necessary, and removing all but beg-of-rnd m on last rnd—16 sts rem.

Next rnd: K2tog 8 times—8 sts rem.

Next rnd: K2tog 4 times—4 sts rem. Cut yarn, draw tail through rem sts, and fasten off inside.

HAT BAND

With smaller needles, CO 12 sts.

Row 1: (RS) Knit.

Row 2: K3, purl to last 3 sts, k3.

Rep Rows 1 and 2 until piece measures 15" (38 cm), ending with a WS row.

Next row: (inc row) K1, k1f&b, knit to end of row—1 st inc'd.

Next row: K3, purl to last 3 sts, k3.

Rep last 2 rows 4 more times—17 sts. Work even for 20 rows.

Next row: (dec row) K1, ssk, knit to end—1 st dec'd.

Next row: K3, purl to last 3 sts, k3.

Rep last 2 rows 4 more times—12 sts rem.

Work even for 4 rows, ending with a WS row. BO all sts.

Weave in loose ends. Using whipstitch (see Glossary, page 131), sew slit closed at base of loop.

felt

With washing machine set to lowest water level, shortest cycle, and hottest temperature, wash the hat. (See page 21 for information on felting.) Check piece for degree of felting every 5 minutes; if necessary, reset the washing machine to begin again, but do not allow the piece to go through a rinse or spin cycle. When it is sufficiently felted, remove the piece from the washer and shape to measurements. Allow to dry completely.

shape

Pull and pinch the turning ridge so that the top of the hat lies flat. Turn hat upside down so crown lies flat. Stuff inside of hat with plastic bags and shape sides level and even. Allow to dry completely.

attach hat band

Insert hat band through back loop with RS facing, lining up shaped edges of bill and band so that ends of band are over the left eye. Pull one end of hat band ½" (1.3 cm) through 1 D-ring and fold end under with wrong sides tog. With thread to match hat and sewing needle, whipstitch hat band to enclose D-ring. Repeat with opposite end and second D-ring. Pin hat band in place on hat. With needle and thread, backstitch edges of hat band to surface of hat, sewing through the felt but not to the interior of the hat.

Thread the silky ribbon through both D-rings and tie in a large bow.

grosgrain ribbon lining

With the iron set to steam, press the grosgrain ribbon, stretching one edge to curve the ribbon into a semicircle. (Although the ribbon is woven and not stretchy, the steam iron will help the ribbon curve.) Take care not to fold the ribbon, because an ironed-in crease cannot be removed. Place label over one end of the grosgrain ribbon so that the top of the label lies along the shorter edge of the ribbon and iron in place.

With hat upside down, locate the lower edge of the center back. Pin label inside hat about ⅛" (3 mm) above the lower edge. Pin ribbon along inside of hat, easing in excess. There should be a bit of slack in the ribbon; distributing it evenly around the inside of the hat allows the brim to stretch slightly when the hat is worn. The ends of the ribbon should just overlap.

Using thread to match ribbon and beg at label, sew ribbon to hat along lower edge as foll: Insert needle through ribbon and hat from wrong side to right side, then insert needle from right side to wrong side above ribbon, making a very small st on right side of hat. Repeat along length of ribbon, making each stitch about ½" (1.3 cm) from previous.

CUSTOM LABELS

The best way to complete your knitting is to create a custom and professional-looking label. It's the signature on your handmade accessory.

Use your computer to create a label about 2¼" (5.5 cm) long and ½" (1.3 cm) wide, leaving 1" (2.5 cm) between labels. This will create about 12 labels per page. Before printing on the silk, print your design on paper to check the orientation and alignment. Follow the directions on the package of silk sheets to get the best quality from your computer.

After the labels have been printed and dried completely, peel off one side of the appliqué paper and position the printed label sheet over it. Smooth out any wrinkles or bubbles. The adhesive paper will adhere to the silk without shifting, but it can be repositioned easily until it is ironed. Use the pinking shears to cut out the labels. Peel off the other side of the appliqué paper and attach each label to the grosgrain ribbon, leaving about ¾" (2 cm) between labels. Iron to secure and cut the ribbon with the pinking shears.

YOU WILL NEED:

8½ × 11" Jacquard Inkjet Silk sheets (or other printable silk fabric sheets)

Computer and ink-jet printer

12" (30.5 cm) square Steam a Seam double-sided fusible appliqué adhesive paper

Iron and ironing board

Spool of 1" (2.5 cm) wide grosgrain ribbon

Pinking shears

RUFFLED
NECK
KERCHIEF

Treat yourself to a kerchief worked
in soft buttery alpaca. A simple mix
of chevron lace and effortless color
changes makes this a lovely first lace
pattern. Asymmetrical ruffles are added
at the end for a sweet finish. Fold the
kerchief diagonally and wrap around
your neck, tying in back.

finished size
21" (53.5 cm) wide and 20"
(51 cm) long, excluding ruffle.

yarn
Sportweight (Fine #2).
Shown here: Blue Sky Alpacas
Royal (100% alpaca; 288 yd
[263 m]/100 g): #702 Spanish
leather (light brown) and #705
antique black (dark brown), 1
skein each.

needles
U.S. size 3 (3.25 mm). Adjust
needle size if necessary to obtain
the correct gauge.

notions
Locking-ring marker; tapestry
needle.

gauge
24½ sts and 42 rows = 4" (10 cm)
in patt st.

construction
The lace kerchief is worked in a
square, changing colors at the
midpoint. After main piece is
completed, stitches are picked up
across one side and bound-off
edge for ruffles.

KERCHIEF

With light brown, CO 129 sts.

Row 1: (RS) Knit.
Row 2 and all even-numbered rows: Purl.
Row 3: K2, *p1, k1; rep from * to last 3 sts, p1, k2.
Row 5: K2, p1, k3, *k2tog, yo, k1, yo, sl 1, k1, psso, k2; rep from * to last 4 sts, k1, p1, k2.
Row 7: K2, p1, k2, *k2tog, yo, k3, yo, sl 1, k1, psso; rep from * to last 5 sts, k2, p1, k2.
Row 8: Purl.

Rep Rows 5–8 until piece measures 12" (30.5 cm) from CO, ending with Row 8.

*Change to dark brown and work Rows 5–8 three times.
Change to light brown and work Rows 5–8 once more.
Rep from * 2 more times.

Change to dark brown and rep Rows 5–8 until piece measures 20" (51 cm) from CO, ending with Row 8.

Work Row 3 once.
Work Row 2 once.
BO all sts.

RUFFLES

ruffle 1

With RS facing, dark brown, and beg at start of first dark brown stripe, pick up and knit 60 sts along right selvedge to BO edge.

Row 1: (WS) Purl.
Row 2: *P1, yo, k3; rep from * to end—75 sts.
Row 3: *P4, k1; rep from * to end.
Row 4: *P1, yo, k4; rep from * to end—90 sts.
Row 5: *P5, k1; rep from * to end.
Row 6: *P1, yo, k5; rep from * to end—105 sts.
Row 7: *P6, k1; rep from * to end.
Row 8: *P1, yo, k6; rep from * to end—120 sts.
Row 9: *P7, k1; rep from * to end.
Row 10: *P1, yo, k7; rep from * to end—135 sts.
Row 11: *P8, k1; rep from * to end.
BO all sts in patt.

ruffle 2

Beg at selvedge edge of ruffle 1, measure 13" (33 cm) across edge of ruffle and BO edge of kerchief and place locking-ring marker to indicate 13" (33 cm) point.

With RS facing and dark brown, beg at end of ruffle 1, pick up and knit 76 sts to marker.

Row 1: (WS) Purl.
Row 2: *K3, yo, p1; rep from * to end—95 sts.
Row 3: *K1, p4; rep from * to end.
Row 4: *K4, yo, p1; rep from * to end—114 sts.
Row 5: *K1, p5; rep from * to end.
Row 6: *K5, yo, p1; rep from * to end—133 sts.
Row 7: *K1, p6; rep from * to end.
Row 8: *K6, yo, p1; rep from * to end—152 sts.
Row 9: *K1, p7; rep from * to end.
Row 10: *K7, yo, p1; rep from * to end—171 sts.
Row 11: *K1, p8; rep from * to end.
Row 12: *K8, yo, p1; rep from * to end—190 sts.
Row 13: *K1, p9; rep from * to end.
Row 14: *K9, yo, p1; rep from * to end—209 sts.
Row 15: *K1, p10; rep from * to end.
BO all sts in patt.

Weave in loose ends and block lightly.

BAMBOO DIAMOND SHELL

Over the last few years the fashion industry has embraced handwork such as embroidery, macramé, and quilting, which has resulted in some beautiful and inspiring design. My choice of diamond pattern for this sweater was a tribute to quilts and quilting.

finished size
29¾ (36, 42¼)" (75.5 [91.5, 107.5 cm) bust circumference. Shell shown measures 29¾" (75.5 cm).

yarn
Worsted weight (Medium #4). *Shown here:* South West Trading Company Bamboo (100% bamboo; 250 yd [229 m]/100 g): #150 brown, 3 (4, 5) balls.

needles
U.S. size 5 (3.75 mm): 24" (60 cm) circular (cir) and set of 4 or 5 double-pointed (dpn). U.S. size 6 (4 mm): 16" and 24" (40 and 60 cm) cir. Adjust needle size if necessary to obtain the correct gauge.

notions
2 large stitch holders; markers (m); locking-ring marker; tapestry needle; one 1⅛" (3 cm) button; sewing needle and matching thread.

gauge
23 sts and 30 rows = 4" (10 cm) in diamond patt on larger needle; 21 sts and 33 rows = 4" (10 cm) in St st on larger needle.

construction
The body is knitted in the round in one piece beginning at the waist edge. The front and back are divided to work increases for the arm openings. The piece is rejoined in the round to continue working body and yoke. The waistband and collar are worked separately and attached, and stitches are picked up for the cuffs.

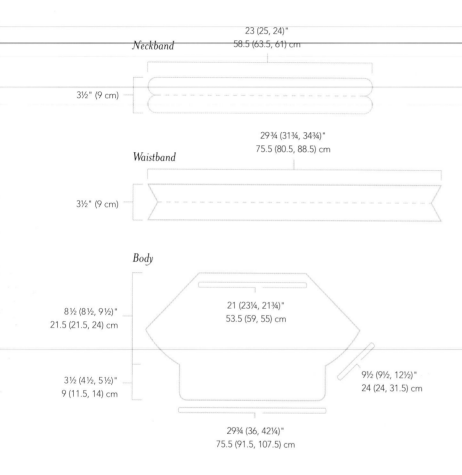

Neckband

23 (25, 24)"
58.5 (63.5, 61) cm

3½" (9 cm)

Waistband

29¾ (31¾, 34¾)"
75.5 (80.5, 88.5) cm

3½" (9 cm)

Body

8½ (8½, 9½)"
21.5 (21.5, 24) cm

21 (23¼, 21¾)"
53.5 (59, 55) cm

3½ (4½, 5½)"
9 (11.5, 14) cm

9½ (9½, 12½)"
24 (24, 31.5) cm

29¾ (36, 42¼)"
75.5 (91.5, 107.5) cm

Diamond Chart

			7
			5
			3
			1

☐ k on RS; p on WS

• p on RS; k on WS

☐ pattern repeat

BODY

With smaller cir needle, CO 152 (184, 216) sts. Place marker (pm) and join for working in the rnd, being careful not to twist sts.

Rnds I and 2: Knit.

Rnd 3: (inc rnd) *K7, k1f&b; rep from * 18 (22, 26) more times—171 (207, 243) sts.

Change to larger needle and work Rows I–8 of Diamond chart 3 (4, 5) times.

back & sleeves

Row I: (WS) With WS facing, use the knitted method (see Glossary, page 127) to CO 9 sts for sleeve, knit these 9 sts, work Row 1 of Diamond chart 9 (11, 13) times, place next 90 (108, 126) sts on holder—90 (108, 126) sts rem for back.

Rows 2–6 (2–6, 2–8): Using the knitted method, CO 9 sts for sleeve, work next row of chart to end of row—135 (153, 189) sts after Row 6 (6, 8).

Place sts on a holder and cut yarn. Mark back with a locking-ring marker to distinguish it from front.

front and sleeves

Replace 90 (108, 126) held sts onto larger needle and rejoin yarn.

Row 1: (RS) Using the knitted method, CO 9 sts, work Row 1 of Diamond chart to end of row—99 (117, 135) sts.

Rows 2–6 (2–6, 2–8): Using the knitted method, CO 9 sts, work next row of chart to end of row—144 (162, 198) sts after Row 6 (6, 8).

rejoin front and back

Next rnd: With RS of front facing, work Row 7 (7, 1) of chart across 144 (162, 198) front sts, pm, work Row 7 (7, 1) of chart across 135 (153, 189) back sts from holder—279 (315, 387) sts. Pm and join for working in the rnd.

Next rnd: Work Row 8 (8, 2) of chart.

Work Rows 1–8 (1–8, 3–8) of chart once, then work Rows 1–8 three (three, four) times, then work Row 1 once more.

yoke

Setup rnd: Knit, dec 4 (10, 7) sts evenly spaced—275 (305, 380) sts rem.

Rnd 1: [K3, k2tog] 55 (61, 76) times—220 (244, 304) sts rem.

Rnds 2–6: Knit.

Rnd 7: [K2, k2tog] 55 (61, 76) times—165 (183, 228) sts rem.

Rnds 8–13: Knit.

Rnd 14: [K1 (1, 0), k2tog] 55 (61, 114) times—110 (122, 114) sts rem.

Rnds 15–24: Knit.

BO all sts loosely.

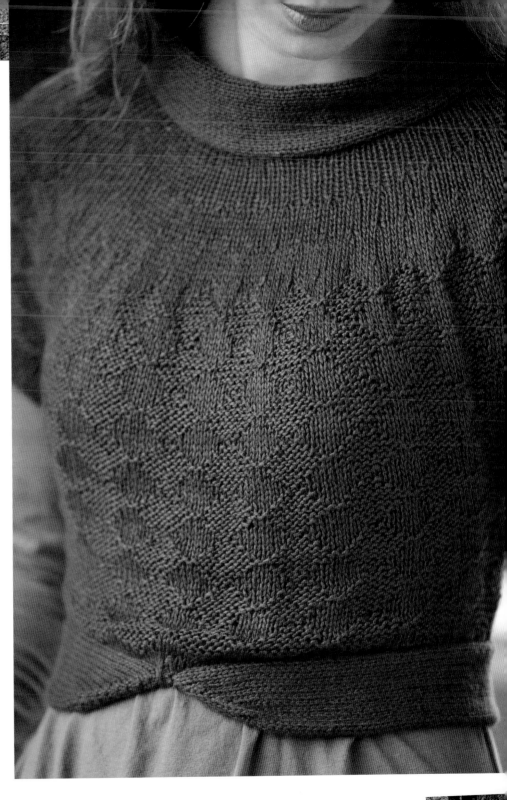

WAISTBAND

With smaller needle, CO 5 sts.

Row 1: K1, k1f&b, knit to end of row—1 st inc'd.

Row 2: Purl.

Rep Rows 1 and 2 six more times—12 sts. Place sts on holder.

With smaller needle, CO 5 sts.

Row 1: (RS) Knit to last 2 sts, k1f&b, k1—1 st inc'd.

Row 2: Purl.

Rep Rows 1 and 2 six more times—12 sts.

Next row: K12, k12 from holder—24 sts.

Work in St st until piece measures 28 (30, 33)" (71 [76, 84] cm) from CO or 1¾" (4.5 cm) less than desired finished waist, ending with a WS row.

shape waistband taper

Row 1: (dec row) K9, k2tog, k1, place next 12 sts on holder—11 sts rem.

Row 2: Purl.

Row 3: Knit to last 3 sts, k2tog, k1—1 st dec'd.

Row 4: Purl.

Rep Rows 3 and 4 four more times—6 sts rem.

Next row: (bind-off row) BO 2 sts, k2tog, pass st over k2tog to BO 1 st, k1, pass k2tog over knit st to BO 1 st. Fasten off last st—no sts rem.

Place 12 held sts onto smaller needle.

Row 1: (RS) K1, ssk, knit to end—1 st dec'd.

Row 2: Purl.

Rep Rows 1 and 2 five more times—6 sts rem.

Next row: (bind-off row) K1, ssk, pass knit st over ssk to BO 1 st, BO all sts to end of row. Fasten off last st—no sts rem.

NECKBAND

With smaller needle, CO 6 sts.

Row 1: K1, k1f&b, k2, k1f&b, k1—8 sts.
Row 2 and all WS rows: Purl.
Row 3: K1, k1f&b, k4, k1f&b, k1—10 sts.
Row 5: K1, k1f&b, k6, k1f&b, k1—12 sts.
Row 6: Purl.

Place sts on holder. Make a second piece to match, but do not place sts on holder.

Next row: K12, k12 held sts—24 sts.
Next row: Purl.
Next row: (buttonhole row) K4, BO 4 sts, knit to last 8 sts, BO 4 sts, knit to end—16 sts rem.
Next row: P4, using the knitted method, CO 4 sts, p8, using the knitted method, CO 4 sts, p4—24 sts.

Work in St st until piece measures 22 (24, 23)" (56 [61, 58.5] cm) from CO, ending with a WS row.

shape neckband point

Row 1: K1, ssk, k6, k2tog, k1, place next 12 sts on holder—10 sts rem.
Row 2: Purl.
Row 3: K1, ssk, k4, k2tog, k1—8 sts rem.
Row 4: Purl.
Row 5: (bind-off row) K1, ssk, pass knit st over ssk to BO 1 st, BO all sts to last 3 sts, k2tog, pass st over k2tog to BO 1 st, k1, pass k2tog over knit st to BO 1 st. Fasten off last st—no sts rem.

Place 12 held sts onto smaller needle and rep Rows 1–5.

FINISHING

Weave in loose ends.

attach waistband

Fold waistband lengthwise with WS tog. With yarn threaded on a tapestry needle, use mattress st (see Glossary, page 131) to join front and back of taper at end of band tog, leaving a slight opening at each point. Mark lower front center of sweater. Pin waistband around bottom edge of sweater with tapered ends meeting at front center. Use mattress st to sew RS of sweater to RS of one long edge of band, easing in fabric as needed. Use whipstitch (see Glossary, page 131) to sew other long edge of waistband to CO edge on WS of sweater.

attach neckband

Fold neckband lengthwise with WS tog. Use mattress st to sew front and back of pointed end of band tog. Pin buttonhole end of neckband to right front so that CO edge of band is even with edge of sweater. Pin neckband around neck opening, lapping end of neckband under buttonhole. Use mattress st and whipstitch to sew neckband to neck opening as for waistband, leaving pointed ends loose. Sew button to BO end of neckband behind buttonhole.

cuffs

With RS facing and dpn, pick up and knit 57 (57, 75) sts along CO edge around entire armhole opening. Pm and join for working in the rnd. Knit 9 rnds. Purl 1 rnd (turning ridge). Knit 9 rnds. BO all sts very loosely. Turn cuff band under along purl row. Whipstitch BO edge of cuff band to CO edge of arm opening. Rep for other armhole opening.

PLEATED
DENIM
PURSE

For those times you only need to keep a few essentials with you, this tiny purse fits the bill. Hang it from your wrist with a little chain handle and learn a few beading skills to attach your chosen charms. Line your bag for extra structure and security.

finished size
6½" (16.5 cm) tall, 7¼" (18.5 cm) wide, 3¾" (9.5 cm) flap length before washing; 5¾" (14.5 cm) tall, 7¼" (18.5 cm) wide, 3¼" (8.5 cm) flap length after washing.

yarn
Worsted weight (Medium #4). *Shown here:* Rowan Denim (100% cotton; 102 yd [93 m]/50 g): #225 Nashville (dark blue) or #324 ecru (cream), 1 skein.

needles
U.S. size 5 (3.75 mm). Adjust needle size if necessary to obtain the correct gauge.

notions
Cable needle (cn); six ½–⅝" (1.3–1.5 cm) buttons; sewing needle and thread; ¼ yd (.25 m) lining fabric; fabric pencil; sewing machine (optional). *Jewelry materials (optional):* 16mm gold-tone base metal clip; 1 ft (30.5 cm) gold-plated steel chain; 1" (2.5 cm) of 1 mm gold-tone chain; two 2" (5 cm) pieces of fine gold-tone wire; 2 gold-tone jump rings; one 6 mm raku square metallic bead; one 10 mm raku round metallic bead; one 8 mm raku round metallic bead; one 9 mm square wooden bead; one ⅞" (2.2 cm) white conch shell; 4½" (11.5 cm) of 1.25 mm leather lacing; wire cutters; round-nose pliers; flat-nose pliers.

gauge
22 sts and 30 rows = 4" (10 cm) in St st before washing; 22 sts and 34 rows = 4" (10 cm) in St st after washing.

construction
The purse is worked in 2 pieces, one front and one back with attached flap.

PURSE FRONT

CO 14 sts.

Row 1: (RS) Purl.

Row 2: Knit.

Row 3: Using the knitted method (see Glossary, page 131), CO 3 sts, k3 CO sts, p14—17 sts.

Row 4: CO 3 sts, p3 CO sts, k14, p3—20 sts.

CO 3 sts at beg of next 4 rows, working CO sts in St st and maintaining 14 center sts in rev St st—32 sts.

CO 2 sts at beg of foll 4 rows, working CO sts in St st and maintaining 14 center sts in rev St st—40 sts.

Inc row: (RS) K1, k1f&b, work in patt to last 2 sts, k1f&b, k1—2 sts inc'd.

Cont in patt as established, rep inc row every RS row 3 more times—48 sts.
Work 7 rows even in patt.
Work in rev St st for 18 rows.

pleat

Next row: (RS) P10, sl 7 sts to cn and hold in front of next 7 sts on left needle, [purl 1 st from left needle and 1 st from cn tog] 7 times, sl 7 sts to cn and hold in back of next 7 sts on left needle, [purl 1 st from cn and 1 st from left needle tog] 7 times, purl to end of row—34 sts rem.

Work 3 rows in rev St st.
BO all sts pwise.

BACK AND FLAP

Work as for front to last row but do not BO sts.

Next row: BO 10 sts purlwise, knit to last 10 sts, BO 10 sts purlwise—14 sts rem. Cut yarn.

With WS facing, rejoin yarn and purl 1 row.

Next row: (RS) K1, p1, knit to last 2 sts, p1, k1.

Next row: P1, k1, purl to last 2 sts, k1, p1.

Rep last 2 rows once more.

Next row: K1, p1, M1, knit to last 2 sts, M1, p1, k1—2 sts inc'd.
Work 1 row even in patt.
Rep last 2 rows 2 more times—20 sts.

Next row: (buttonhole row) K1, p1, M1, k1, yo, k2tog, knit to last 4 sts, yo, k2tog, M1, p1, k1—22 sts.
Work 5 rows even in patt as established.

Next row: (buttonhole row) K1, p1, k1, yo, k2tog, knit to last 4 sts, yo, k2tog, p1, k1. Work 1 row even in patt as established.

decrease section

Row 1: (dec row) K1, p1, ssk, knit to last 4 sts, k2tog, p1, k1— 2 sts dec'd.

Row 2: Work even in patt as established. Rep Rows 1 and 2 two more times—16 sts rem.

Next row: (buttonhole row) K1, p1, k1, ssk, yo, k2tog, knit to last 6 sts, yo, [k2tog] 2 times, p1, k1—14 sts rem.
Work 1 row even in patt as established.

Next row: (bind-off row) Ssk, BO all sts to last 2 sts, k2tog, BO last st—no sts rem.

Lining of bag

FINISHING

With yarn threaded on a tapestry needle and WS tog, use mattress stitch (see Glossary, page 131) to join sides and bottom of front and back. Weave in loose ends. Machine wash in warm water and tumble dry. Reblock if needed using a damp towel.

With sewing needle and thread, attach buttons to front beneath buttonholes.

lining

Fold lining fabric in half with RS tog. Lay finished bag on top of lining fabric. With fabric pencil, outline bag and add ½" (1.3 cm) on all sides. Cut through both layers to make two lining pieces.

With sewing machine or needle and thread, turn top edge of lining under ½" (1.3 cm) and hem (see sewing information, page 75). With RS tog, sew lining pieces together at sides and bottom, using ½" (1.3 cm) seam allowance. Finish cut edges. Sew lining to bag at bag opening.

DETACHABLE CHARM CHAIN HANDLE (*optional*)

make charms

String conch on one piece of gold wire and attach to chain by making a wire bail (see opposite). String 10 mm raku bead on second piece of gold wire and make a wire bail. Use a jump ring to attach the wrapped loop to the fine chain (see opposite). Attach the other end of the fine chain to the large chain with the other jump ring. Tie an overhand knot in the leather lacing about ¾" (2 cm) from one end. String 8 mm raku bead and wooden bead. Pass leather lacing through last link of large chain and string 6 mm raku bead. Tie an overhand knot in the other end of the lacing, leaving a 2¼" (5.5 cm) tail and trapping the heavier gold chain loosely between the wooden and raku beads.

attach chain to purse

Squeeze and twist the base-metal clip open and pass through 2 sts on side seam at top of bag. String the last link of the gold chain (the end nearest the charms), and string 1 link about 1½" (3.8 cm) from the other end of the chain. Close the clip. The charms and chain should hang in a cluster at the side of the bag.

JEWELRY TOOLS

The pliers and wire cutters used in jewelry resemble the hardware store variety, but they're smoother, smaller, and better suited to more delicate wirework. The most common jewelry tools include the following.

Wire cutters have sharp jaws to cut beading wire.

Round-nose pliers have tapered cone-shaped jaws for making loops.

Flat-nose pliers have flat tapered jaws to hold wire steady.

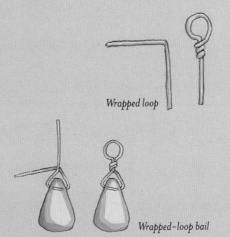

Wrapped loop

Wrapped-loop bail

JEWELRY TECHNIQUES

Wrapped loops look elegant, are secure, and don't snag. To create a wrapped loop, make a 90° bend in the wire 2" (5 cm) from one end. Use the round-nose pliers to hold the wire near the bend, then wrap the short end of wire up and around the pliers until the short end crosses the long end. Wrap the short end tightly down the neck of the wire several times to create a couple of coils. Trim the excess short tail close with wire cutters.

Bails turn side-drilled beads into pendants. Center the bead on a piece of wire. Bend both ends of the wire up the sides and across the top of the bead. Bend one end straight up at the center of the bead and wrap the other wire around it a few times. Form a wrapped loop with the straight-up wire, wrapping it back down over the already-formed coils. Trim the excess wire.

SOFT KID BUBBLE

The bubble shape has made a permanent home in my wardrobe. I love the wearability of something snug on top and loose on the bottom to layer over leggings or denim. The open lace panel across the chest gives a Scandinavian-inspired touch, and the soft mohair yarn keeps this piece light, not bulky.

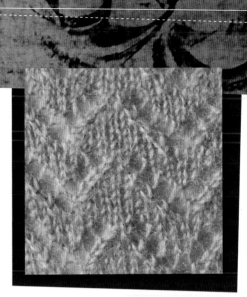

finished size
35¾ (40, 44¼)" (91 [101.5, 112.5] cm) bust circumference. Dress shown measures 35¾" (91 cm).

yarn
Sportweight (Fine #2).
Shown here: GGH Soft Kid (70% mohair, 25% nylon, 5% wool; 150 yd [137 m]/25 g): #58 sea green, 6 (7, 9) balls.

needles
U.S. size 5 (3.75 mm): 24" (60 cm) circular (cir). U.S. size 6 (4 mm): straight and 24" (60 cm) cir. Adjust needle size if necessary to obtain the correct gauge.

notions
2 large stitch holders; 3 small stitch holders; 4 markers (m), 1 in a different color; cable needle (cn); tapestry needle; size G/6 (4 mm) crochet hook.

gauge
23 sts and 31 rows = 4" (10 cm) in St st on larger needle.

construction
The piece is worked in the round from the bottom up, then the front and back are divided and the front stitches held. The insides of the pockets are knitted separately and attached to the sides of the back so that they wrap around the hip. Setting aside the back and pockets, the front and pocket openings are worked back and forth. The front, back, and pockets are rejoined to work in the round through the lace and bust section, then divided to work the armholes and neck opening.

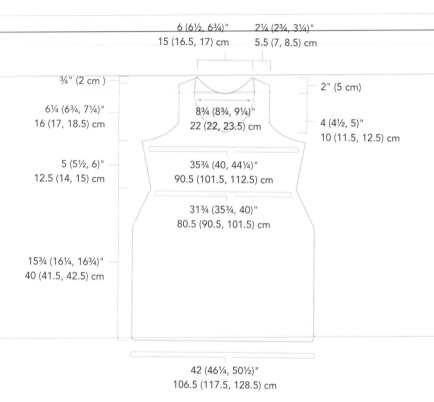

6 (6½, 6¾)"
15 (16.5, 17) cm

2¼ (2¾, 3¼)"
5.5 (7, 8.5) cm

¾" (2 cm)

6¼ (6¾, 7¼)"
16 (17, 18.5) cm

8¾ (8¾, 9¼)"
22 (22, 23.5) cm

2" (5 cm)

4 (4½, 5)"
10 (11.5, 12.5) cm

5 (5½, 6)"
12.5 (14, 15) cm

35¾ (40, 44¼)"
90.5 (101.5, 112.5) cm

31¾ (35¾, 40)"
80.5 (90.5, 101.5) cm

15¾ (16¼, 16¾)"
40 (41.5, 42.5) cm

42 (46¼, 50½)"
106.5 (117.5, 128.5) cm

BODY

With smaller needle, CO 242 (266, 290) sts. Place marker (pm) and join for working in the rnd, being careful not to twist sts.

Work in k1, p1 rib for 2" (5 cm). Change to larger needle and work in St st until piece measures 9½ (10, 10½)" (24 [25.5, 26.5] cm) from CO. Place first 10 sts on holder for top of left pocket, place next 101 (113, 125) sts on holder for front, place next 10 sts on holder for top

of right pocket, leave next 121 (133, 145) sts on needle for back. Set aside.

POCKETS

With larger straight needles, CO 42 sts. Work in St st for 2½" (6.5 cm), ending with a WS row. Place sts on a holder and cut yarn.

Make second pocket to match, but do not place sts on holder and do not cut yarn.

attach pockets

With RS facing and larger cir needle, k42 pocket sts, pm of different color, k121 (133, 145) back sts, pm, k42 pocket sts from holder—205 (217, 229) sts total.

Working back and forth in rows, work in St st until piece measures 2¼" (5.5 cm) from pocket attachment, ending with a WS row.

shape waist

Row 1: (RS) K40, k2tog, sl m, k1, pm, ssk, knit to 3 sts before m, k2tog, pm, k1, sl m, ssk, k40—201 (213, 225) sts rem.

Row 2: Purl.

Row 3: (dec row) Knit to 2 sts before m, k2tog, k1, ssk, knit to 2 sts before m, k2tog, k1, ssk, knit to end of row—4 sts dec'd.

Row 4: Purl.

Rep last 2 rows 13 more times—145 (157, 169) sts rem.

Place pocket and back sts on holder, leaving markers in place.

shape pocket opening

Row 1: (RS) With larger cir needle and RS facing, k101 (113, 125) front sts from holder.

Row 2: Purl.

Row 3: (dec row) K1, ssk, knit to last 3 sts, k2tog, k1—2 sts dec'd.
Working in St st, rep dec row every other row 5 more times, then every 4th row once, then every 6th row 5 times—77 (89, 101) sts rem.

join front, back, and pockets

Next row: With larger cir needle (holding front sts) and RS facing, using yarn attached to front, k138 (150, 162) pocket and back sts from holder, place next 7 sts from holder onto cn and hold in back of first 7 front sts, [knit 1 front st tog with 1 st from cn] 7 times, k63 (75, 87) front sts, place next 7 front sts onto cn and hold in front of next 7 sts on left needle, [knit 1 st from cn tog with 1 st from left needle] 7 times, k20 to arrive at beg of rnd—208 (232, 256) sts rem; different-colored m marks beg of rnd.

Next rnd: (pleat rnd) K1 side st, k89 (101, 113) back sts, k1 side st, k32 (38, 44) front sts, *place next 4 sts onto cn and hold in back of next 4 sts on left needle, [knit 1 st from left needle tog with 1 st from cn] 4 times; rep from * once more, place next 5 sts onto cn and hold in back of next 5 sts on left needle, [knit 1 st from left needle tog with 1 st from cn] 5 times, k1, place next 5 sts onto cn and hold in front of next 5 sts on left needle, [knit 1 st from cn tog with 1 st from left needle] 5 times, *place next 4 sts onto cn and hold in front of next 4 sts on left needle, [knit 1 st from cn tog with 1 st from left needle] 4 times; rep from * once more, knit to end of rnd—182 (206, 230) sts rem; 91 (103, 115) sts for front, 89 (101, 113) sts for back, and 1 st at each side between markers.

Knit 2 (6, 10) rnds even.

shape bust and work lace pattern

Rnd 1: (inc rnd 1) K1, k1f&b, knit to 1 st before m, k1f&b, k1, k1f&b, k31 (37, 43), pm for beg of lace patt, work Row 1 of Lace chart 3 times, pm for end of lace patt, k31 (37, 43), k1f&b—186 (210, 234) sts.

Rnd 2: Knit, working Row 2 of chart between m.

Rnd 3: (inc rnd 2) K1, k1f&b, knit to 1 st before m, k1f&b, k1, k1f&b, knit to m, work next row of chart to m, knit to 1 st before m, k1f&b—4 sts inc'd.

Working in St st, rep inc rnd 2 every other rnd once more, then every 4th rnd 3 times—206 (230, 254) sts; Row 1 of 3rd rep of chart is complete. Work even, working Rows 2–8 of chart, then Rows 1–8, then Rows 1–5—4 full reps of chart, plus 5 rows of 5th rep complete.

front

Place first 103 (115, 127) sts (101 [113, 125] back sts plus 2 side sts) on large holder—103 (115, 127) sts rem for front.

Purl 1 WS row.

Next row: (RS) K1, ssk, knit to m, work Row 7 of chart, knit to last 3 sts, k2tog, k1—101 (113, 125) sts rem.

Purl 1 row.

BO 2 sts at beg of next 4 rows—93 (105, 117) sts rem.

shape left neck and armhole

BO 2 sts, knit until there are 25 (31, 37) sts on right needle, place next 39 sts on holder for front neck, and place foll 27 (33, 39) sts on holder for right front—25 (31, 37) sts rem.

Working in St st, BO 2 sts at beg of next 2 RS rows, then dec 1 st at armhole edge every RS row 2 (5, 7) times and *at the same time* dec 1 st at neck edge every RS row 6 (6, 7) times—13 (16, 19) sts rem when all shaping is complete. Work even until armhole measures 6¼ (6¾, 7¼)" (16 [17, 18.5] cm), ending with a WS row.

shape left shoulder

BO 5 (6, 7) sts at beg of next RS row, then BO 4 (5, 6) sts at beg of foll 2 RS rows.

shape right neck and armhole

With RS facing, keeping 39 sts at center front on holder, rejoin yarn to 27 (33, 39) right front sts and knit to end of row.

Working in St st, BO 2 sts at beg of next 3 WS rows, then dec 1 st at armhole edge every RS row 2 (5, 7) times and *at the same time* dec 1 st at neck edge every RS row 6 (6, 7) times—13 (16, 19) sts rem when all shaping is complete. Work even until armhole measures 6¼ (6¾, 7¼)" (16 [17, 18.5] cm), ending with a RS row.

Lace Chart

\	O					O	/	7
	\	O			O	/		5
		\	O	O	/			3
			\	O				1

☐ k on RS; p on WS

O yo

/ k2tog

\ ssk

☐ pattern repeat

shape right shoulder

BO 5 (6, 7) sts at beg of next WS row, then BO 4 (5, 6) sts at beg of foll 2 WS rows.

back

Place 103 (115, 127) back sts from holder onto larger needle and rejoin yarn.

Next row: (RS) K1, ssk, knit to last 3 sts, k2tog, k1—101 (113, 125) sts rem.

Purl 1 WS row.

BO 2 sts at beg of next 20 (22, 24) rows—61 (69, 77) sts rem. Work even until armhole measures 5 (5½, 6)" (12.5 [14, 15] cm), ending with a WS row.

shape right back neck

Next row: (RS) K18 (21, 24), place next 25 (27, 29) sts on holder for back neck, and place foll 18 (21, 24) sts on holder for left back—18 (21, 24) sts rem.

Working in St st, BO 2 sts at beg of next 2 WS rows, then BO 1 st at beg of foll WS row—13 (16, 19) sts rem. Work even in St st until armhole measures 6¼ (6¾, 7¼)" (16 [17, 18.5] cm), ending with a WS row.

shape right shoulder

BO 5 (6, 7) sts at beg of next RS row,

then BO 4 (5, 6) sts at beg of foll 2 RS rows.

shape left back neck
Keeping 25 (27, 29) sts at center back on holder, rejoin yarn to 18 (21, 24) left back sts and knit to end of row.

Working in St st, BO 2 sts at beg of next 2 RS rows, then BO 1 st at beg of foll RS row—13 (16, 19) sts rem. Work even in St st until armhole measures 6¼ (6¾, 7¼)" (16 [17, 18.5] cm), ending with a RS row.

shape left shoulder
BO 5 (6, 7) sts at beg of next WS row, then BO 4 (5, 6) sts at beg of foll 2 WS rows.

FINISHING
Weave in loose ends.

rolled collar
With yarn threaded on a tapestry needle, use mattress stitch (see Glossary, page 131) to sew shoulder seams.

With smaller needle and RS facing, k25 (27, 29) from back holder, pick up and knit 15 sts along left back neck edge, 30 (33, 36) sts along left front neck edge, k39 held front neck sts, pick up and knit 30 (33, 36) sts along right front neck edge, 15 sts along

right back neck edge, pm and join for working in the rnd—154 (162, 170) sts total. Work in St st for 13 rnds. BO all sts.

armholes
Beg at base of armhole, single crochet (sc; see Glossary, page 128, for crochet instructions) around entire armhole, join with slip st in first sc. Fasten off.

pockets
right pocket edging
Row 1: With smaller needle and RS facing, pick up and knit 43 sts along right pocket opening, [k1, p1] 4 times across held sts, k2—53 sts total.
Row 2: P2, k1, *p1, k1; rep from * to last 2 sts, p2.
Row 3: K2, p1, *k1, p1; rep from * to last 2 sts, k2.
BO all sts in patt.

With yarn threaded on a tapestry needle, whipstitch (see Glossary, page 131) selvedge edges of edging to body.

left pocket edging
Replace 10 held sts on smaller needle.

Row 1: K2, *p1, k1; rep from * 3 more times, pick up and knit 43

sts along left pocket opening—53 sts total.
Row 2: P2, k1, *p1, k1; rep from * to last 2 sts, p2.
Row 3: K2, p1, *k1, p1; rep from * to last 2 sts, k2.
BO all sts in patt.

With yarn threaded on a tapestry needle, whipstitch selvedge edges of edging to body.

close pockets
With WS of dress facing, pin pockets in place on WS. With yarn threaded on a tapestry needle, carefully whipstitch around right, left, and bottom of each pocket.

BEADED FAIR ISLE HAT

Silk and alpaca are a dreamy combination in this graphic hat. After knitting is completed, deep and shimmery hematite-colored beads are placed precisely at the middle of the Fair Isle section for an elegant accent that contrasts with the softness of the fabric.

finished size
20¼" (51.5 cm) circumference; to fit a woman's medium.

yarn
Worsted weight (Medium #4). *Shown here:* Debbie Bliss Alpaca Silk (80% alpaca, 20% silk; 71 yd [65 m]/50 g): #22 yellow, #26 dark gray, and #13 pale gray, 1 skein each.

needles
U.S. size 6 (4 mm): 16" (40 cm) circular (cir) and set of 4 or 5 double-pointed (dpn). U.S. size 9 (5.5 mm): 16" (40 cm) cir. Adjust needle sizes if necessary to obtain the correct gauge.

notions
Marker (m); twelve 12 mm round faceted hematite beads; sewing needle and matching thread; tapestry needle.

gauge
21 sts and 26 rows = 4" (10 cm) in rib patt on smaller needles. 19 sts and 18 rows = 4" (10 cm) in Fair Isle patt on larger needles.

construction
The hat is worked from the ribbed brim to the crown, working the chart over the middle rounds. The beads are sewn on at the end.

Fair Isle Chart

	yellow
	dark gray
	pale gray
	work with dark gray; sew on bead
	pattern repeat

HAT

brim

With smaller cir and yellow, CO 96 sts. Place marker (pm) and join for working in the rnd, being careful not to twist sts.

Rnds 1–15: *K3, p1; rep from * to end. Change to larger cir.

Fair Isle section

Work Rows 1–19 of Fair Isle chart.

crown

Change to smaller cir.

Note: Change to smaller dpns when sts are too tight to work comfortably on cir.

Rnd 1: *K6, k2tog; rep from * to end—84 sts rem.

Rnd 2: Knit.

Rnd 3: *K5, k2tog; rep from * to end—72 sts rem.

Rnd 4: Knit.

Continue to decrease in this manner, working 1 fewer st between decs on each dec rnd and working 1 rnd even between dec rnds, 4 more times—24 sts rem.

Next rnd: *K2tog; rep from * to end—12 sts rem.

Next rnd: *K2tog; rep from * to end—6 sts rem.

Cut yarn, leaving an 8" (20.5 cm) tail. Draw tail through rem sts and fasten off securely inside.

FINISHING
Weave in loose ends and block lightly. With sewing needle and thread, sew beads securely to hat as shown on chart.

beg	begin(s); beginning		sl	slip
BO	bind off		sl st	slip st (slip 1 st pwise unless otherwise indicated)
CC	contrasting color			
cm	centimeter(s)		ssk	slip 2 sts kwise, one at a time, from the left needle to right needle, insert left needle tip through both front loops and knit together from this position (1 st decrease)
cn	cable needle			
CO	cast on			
dec(s)	decrease(s); decreasing			
dpn	double-pointed needles			
foll	follow(s); following			
g	gram(s)			
inc(s)	increase(s); increasing		St st	stockinette stitch
k	knit		tbl	through back loop
k1f&b	knit into the front and back of same st		tog	together
			WS	wrong side
kwise	knitwise, as if to knit		wyb	with yarn in back
m	marker(s)		wyf	with yarn in front
MC	main color		yd	yard(s)
mm	millimeter(s)		yo	yarnover
M1	make one (increase)		*	repeat starting point
p	purl		**	repeat all instructions between asterisks
p1f&b	purl into front and back of same st			
			( )	alternate measurements and/or instructions
patt(s)	pattern(s)			
psso	pass slipped st over		[ ]	work instructions as a group a specified number of times
pwise	purlwise, as if to purl			
rem	remain(s); remaining			
rep	repeat(s); repeating			
rev St st	reverse stockinette stitch			
rnd(s)	round(s)			
RS	right side			

BIND-OFF
standard bind-off (BO)

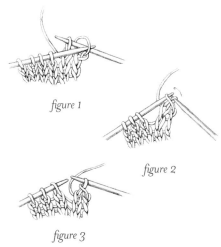

figure 1

figure 2

figure 3

Knit the first stitch, *knit the next stitch (2 stitches on right needle), insert left needle tip into first stitch on right needle (**Figure 1**) and lift this stitch up and over the second stitch (**Figure 2**) and off the needle (**Figure 3**). Repeat from * for the desired number of stitches.

CAST-ONS
backward-loop cast-on

*Loop working yarn and place it on needle backward so that it doesn't unwind. Repeat from *.

cable cast-on

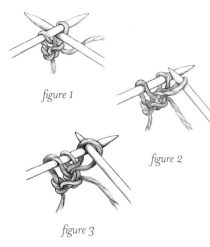

figure 1

figure 2

figure 3

If there are no stitches on the needles, make a slipknot of working yarn and place it on the needle, then use the knitted method to cast-on one more stitch—2 stitches on needle. Hold needle with working yarn in your left hand.

*Insert right needle between the first 2 stitches on left needle (**Figure 1**), wrap yarn around needle as if to knit, draw yarn through (**Figure 2**), and place new loop on left needle (**Figure 3**) to form a new stitch. Repeat from * for the desired number of stitches, always working between the first 2 stitches on the left needle.

knitted cast-on

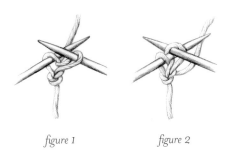

figure 1

figure 2

Make a slipknot of working yarn and place it on the left needle if there are no stitches already there. *Use the right needle to knit the first stitch (or slipknot) on left needle (**Figure 1**) and place new loop onto left needle to form a new stitch (**Figure 2**). Repeat from * for the desired number of stitches, always working into the last stitch made.

long-tail (continental) cast-on

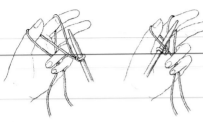

figure 1   *figure 2*

figure 3   *figure 4*

Leaving a long tail (about ½" [1.3 cm] for each stitch to be cast on), make a slipknot and place on right needle. Place thumb and index finger of your left hand between the yarn ends so that working yarn is around your index finger and tail end is around your thumb and secure the yarn ends with your other fingers. Hold your palm upwards, making a V of yarn **(Figure 1)**. *Bring needle up through loop on thumb **(Figure 2)**, catch first strand around index finger, and go back down through loop on thumb **(Figure 3)**. Drop loop off thumb and, placing thumb back in V configuration, tighten resulting stitch on needle **(Figure 4)**. Repeat from * for the desired number of stitches.

CROCHET
crochet chain (ch)

Make a slipknot and place it on crochet hook if there isn't a loop already on the hook. *Yarn over hook and draw through loop on hook. Repeat from * for desired length of chain. To fasten off, cut yarn and draw end through last loop formed.

slip-stitch crochet (sl st)

*Insert hook into a stitch, yarn over hook, and draw a loop through the loop on hook. Repeat from * for the desired number of stitches.

DECREASES
knit 2 together (k2tog)

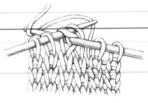

Knit 2 stitches together as if they were a single stitch.

slip, slip, knit (ssk)

figure 1

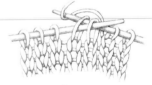

figure 2

Slip 2 stitches individually knitwise **(Figure 1)**, insert left needle tip into the front of these 2 slipped stitches, and use the right needle to knit them together through their back loops **(Figure 2)**.

I-CORD (also called knit-cord)

Using two double-pointed needles, cast on the desired number of stitches (usually 3 to 4). *Without turning the needle, slide stitches to other end of needle, pull the yarn around the back, and knit the stitches as usual. Repeat from * for desired length.

INCREASES
bar increase (k1f&b)

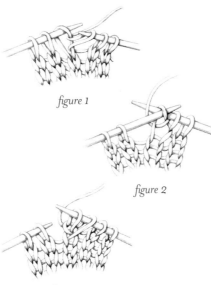

figure 1

figure 2

figure 3

Knit into a stitch but leave it on the left needle **(Figure 1)**, then knit through the back loop of the same stitch **(Figure 2)** and slip the original stitch off the needle **(Figure 3)**.

raised make one (m1)

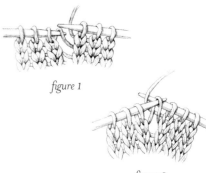

figure 1

figure 2

With left needle tip, lift the strand between the last knitted stitch and the first stitch on the left needle from front to back **(Figure 1)**, then knit the lifted loop through the back **(Figure 2)**.

PICK UP AND KNIT

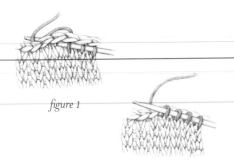

figure 1

figure 2

With right side facing and working from right to left, insert the tip of the needle into the center of the stitch below the bind-off or cast-on edge **(Figure 1)**, wrap yarn around needle, and pull through a loop **(Figure 2)**. Pick up 1 stitch for every bound-off stitch.

figure 3

For shaped edges, insert tip of needle between last and second-to-last stitches, wrap yarn around needle, and pull through a loop **(Figure 3)**. Pick up and knit about 3 stitches for every 4 rows, adjusting as necessary so that picked-up edge lays flat.

SEAMS
backstitch seam

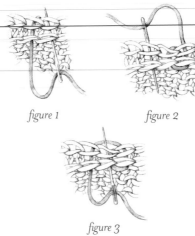

figure 1

figure 2

figure 3

Thread seaming yarn or thread on a needle and join the pieces as follows: Bring threaded needle from back to front between the first 2 stitches on each piece of knitted fabric, then from front to back through both layers 1 stitch to the right of the starting point **(Figure 1)**. *Insert threaded needle through both layers, from back to front, 2 stitches to the left **(Figure 2)**, then from front to back 1 stitch to the right **(Figure 3)**. Repeat from * for desired seam length, working right to left so that seaming yarn follows a circular path.

invisible horizontal seam

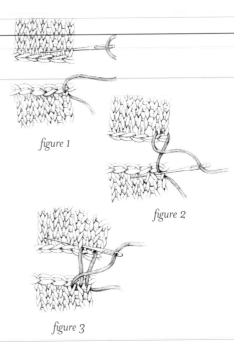

figure 1

figure 2

figure 3

Working with the bound-off edges opposite each other, right sides of the knitting facing you, and working into the stitches just below the bound-off edges, bring threaded tapestry needle out at the center of the first stitch (i.e., go under half of the first stitch) on one side of the seam, then bring needle in and out under the first whole stitch on the other side **(Figure 1)**. *Bring needle into the center of the same stitch it came out of before, then out in the center of the adjacent stitch **(Figure 2)**. Bring needle in and out under the next whole stitch on the other side **(Figure 3)**. Repeat from *, ending with a half-stitch on the first side.

mattress stitch

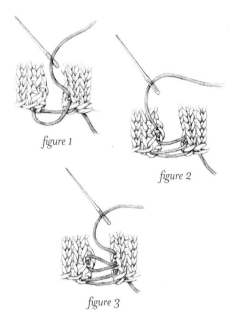

figure 1

figure 2

figure 3

running stitch

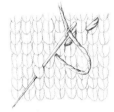

The most common sewing method. Holding the pieces to be joined together, pass a threaded needle from WS to RS and back, creating stitches that look like a small dashed line of equal lengths on both sides.

whipstitch

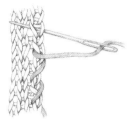

Hold pieces to be sewn together so that the edges to be seamed are even with each other. With yarn threaded on a tapestry needle, *insert needle through both layers from back to front, then bring needle to back. Repeat from *, keeping even tension on the seaming yarn.

Insert threaded needle under 1 bar between the 2 edge stitches on one piece, then under the corresponding bar plus the bar above it on the other piece (Figure 1). *Pick up the next 2 bars on the first piece (Figure 2), then the next 2 bars on the other (Figure 3). Repeat from *, ending by picking up the last bar or pair of bars on the first piece. To reduce bulk in the mattress stitch seam, work as for the 1-stitch seam allowance but pick up the bars in the center of the edge stitches instead of between the last 2 stitches.

SHORT-ROWS
knit side

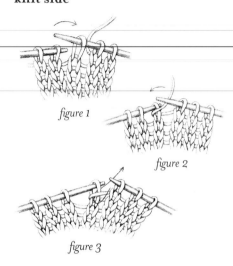

figure 1

figure 2

figure 3

purl side

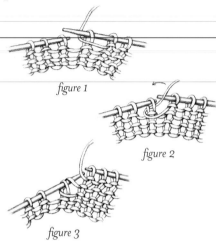

figure 1

figure 2

figure 3

Work to turning point, slip next stitch purlwise (**Figure 1**), bring the yarn to the front, then slip the same stitch back to the left needle (**Figure 2**), turn the work around and bring the yarn in position for the next stitch—1 stitch has been wrapped and the yarn is correctly positioned to work the next stitch. When you come to a wrapped stitch on a subsequent row, hide the wrap by working it together with the wrapped stitch as follows: Insert right needle tip under the wrap (from the front if wrapped stitch is a knit stitch; from the back if wrapped stitch is a purl stitch; **Figure 3**), then into the stitch on the needle, and work the stitch and its wrap together as a single stitch.

Work to the turning point, slip the next stitch purlwise to the right needle, bring the yarn to the back of the work (**Figure 1**), return the slipped stitch to the left needle, bring the yarn to the front between the needles (**Figure 2**), and turn the work so that the knit side is facing—1 stitch has been wrapped and the yarn is correctly positioned to knit the next stitch. To hide the wrap on a subsequent purl row, work to the wrapped stitch, use the tip of the right needle to pick up the wrap from the back, place it on the left needle (**Figure 3**), then purl it together with the wrapped stitch.

TASSEL

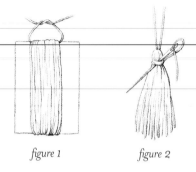

figure 1   *figure 2*

Cut a piece of cardboard 4" (10 cm) wide by the desired length of the tassel plus 1" (2.5 cm). Wrap yarn to desired thickness around cardboard. Cut a short length of yarn and tie tightly around one end of wrapped yarn (**Figure 1**). Cut yarn loops at other end. Cut another piece of yarn and wrap tightly around loops a short distance below top knot to form tassel neck. Knot securely, thread ends onto tapestry needle, and pull to center of tassel (**Figure 2**). Trim ends.

SHOPPING GUIDE

I am ridiculously fortunate to live in Portland, Oregon, a city with so many specialty shops. When looking for unique hardware for a project, I have more than a couple of favorite spots: Oregon Leather Company, which has an overwhelming selection of leather, hardware, and tools; Winks Hardware, an amazing hardware store that you need an escort to explore fully; local fabric stores Josephine's Dry Goods, Fabric Depot, and Bolt, where I love looking for button coverings and lining fabrics; and Button Emporium, a sweet store with a selection of buttons and trims. Explore your own neighborhood for the kind of stores that will inspire you with unexpected and perfect details.

YARNS

Berroco Yarns
PO Box 367
14 Elmdale Rd.
Uxbridge, MA 01569-0367
(508) 278-2527
berroco.com
Ultra Alpaca

Debbie Bliss
Knitting Fever International, distributor
PO Box 336
315 Bayview Ave.
Amityville, NY 11701
(516) 546-3600
knittingfever.com
Alpaca Silk

Blue Sky Alpacas
PO Box 88
Cedar, MN 55011
(888) 460-8862
blueskyalpacas.com
Alpaca Silk, Brushed Suri, Royal, Sport Weight

Brown Sheep Yarns
100662 County Road 16
Mitchell, Nebraska 69357
(800) 826-9136
brownsheep.com
Lamb's Pride Worsted

Classic Elite Yarns
122 Western Ave.
Lowell, MA 01851-1434
(978) 453-2837
classiceliteyarns.com
Lush

GGH Yarns
Muench Yarns, U.S. distributor
1323 Scott St.
Petaluma, CA 94954-1135
(800) 733-9276
muenchyarns.com
Scarlett, Soft Kid, Tajmahal

Elsebeth Lavold
Knitting Fever International, distributor
PO Box 336
315 Bayview Ave.
Amityville, NY 11701
(516) 546-3600
knittingfever.com
Silky Wool

Manos del Uruguay
Fairmount Fibers, distributor
915 N. 28th St.
Philadelphia, PA 19130
(888) 566-9970
fairmountfibers.com
Wool

Mission Falls
CNS Yarns, distributor
5333 Casgrain #1204
Montréal, QC
Canada H2T 1X3
(877) 244-1204
missionfalls.com
1824 Wool

Plymouth Yarns
500 Lafayette St.
Bristol, PA 19007
(215) 788-0459
plymouthyarn.com
Baby Alpaca Grande

Reynolds Yarn
JCA, distributor
35 Scales Ln.
Townsend, MA 01469
(978) 597-8794
jcacrafts.com
Whiskey

Rowan Yarns
Westminster Fibers, U.S. distributor
165 Ledge St.
Nashua, NH 03060
(800) 445-9276
westminsterfibers.com
4-ply Soft, Denim, Kidsilk Night, RYC Soft Lux, Wool Cotton

South West Trading Company
Tempe, AZ
(866) 794-1818
soysilk.com
Bamboo

Twinkle Yarns
Classic Elite Yarns, distributor
122 Western Ave.
Lowell, MA 01851-1434
(978) 453-2837
classiceliteyarns.com
Soft Chunky

Vermont Organic Fiber Co.
52 Seymour St.
Middlebury, VT 05753
(802) 388-1313
vtorganicfiber.com
O-Wool Classic

HARDWARE, NOTIONS, AND ACCESSORIES

Best Felted Collar
Buttons: La Mode hook 622, genuine leather style #622

Softly Pleated Sleeves
Trim: Beaded Victorian "Style" gray trim (Button Emporium)

Sunshine Intarsia Bag
Zipper: Coats and Clark 7–9" (18–23 cm) brass jeans zipper Z40
D-Ring: Large handmade 3" (7.5 cm) brass rigging D-ring (Oregon Leather)
Chicago Screws: ⅜" (1 cm) brass Chicago screws (Oregon Leather)

Half-Felted Bag
Chain: 24" heavy chain (Dava Bead and Trade)
Chicago Screws: ¾" (2 cm) nickel Chicago screws (Oregon Leather)
D-Rings: Dritz #177-34-65, size ¾" (2 cm)
Cord Lock Stops:
Snaps: Sew-on magnetic snaps #BR-1985 (Button Emporium)
Leather Lacing: Gray deer-leather lacing (Oregon Leather)

Raglan Wrap
Buttons: Dritz #355 size 1⅛" (2.9 cm)
Snaps: Dritz size 4 Sew-on snaps

Argyle Lace Hat
Buttons: Dritz Cover Button Kit, size ⅝" (1.5 cm)

Hoodie Devoted
Beads: 1⅛" (3 cm) wooden beads (Dava Bead and Trade)

Heather Headband
Headband: Plastic 1½ × 15" (3.8 × 38 cm) headband (J. Caroline Creative)

Big Brown Bag
Chicago Screws: ¼" (6 mm) nickel Chicago screws (Oregon Leather)
Leather Lacing: 1.25 mm fine European Greek leather lacing (Dava Bead and Trade)
Beads: 1" (2.5 cm) cream woven fabric circular beads (Dava Bead and Trade)
Horseshoe Hooks: 1¼" (3.2 cm) nickel horseshoe handle hook (J. Caroline Creative)

Braided Cable Belt
Buckles: 1 × 1½" (2.5 × 3.8 cm) nickel buckles (Oregon Leather)

Plain Talk Ruffled Mittens
Palms and Thumbs: Fiber Trends Suede 2-Piece Mitten Palms (Fiber Trends)

Whiskey Felted Cap
D-Rings: Dritz ¾" (2 cm) D-rings

Pleated Denim Purse
Handle: All chain, charms, and notions (Dava Bead and Trade)

Beaded Fair Isle Hat
Beads: 12 mm hematite Czech fire-polished beads (Dava Bead and Trade)

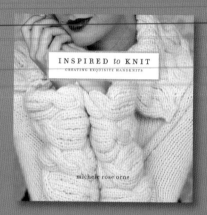